01622001   0?6516

942.41 BRI
BRISTOL BROA
83/6516

D1589113

"Any m̶o̶v̶e̶m̶... ...i̶g̶n̶o̶r̶a̶... ...her of other pe... ...history... We... ...ure unless we keep our hands on our...

Gwyn Williams.

Bristol Broadsides

B.C.H.E. – LIBRARY

00126182

ACKNOWLEDGEMENTS:

Thanks to: City of Bristol Record Office ,
Blaise Castle House Museum,
Workers' Educational Association,
Chief Environmental Health Officer (Bristol),
Bristol May Day Committee,
Avon County Reference Library,
South West Arts,
Fred Lancaster,
Will Guy,
Phil Chapman,
Sarah Braun,
Beryl Begley,
Rose Prewett.

Produced by: Bristol Broadsides (Co-op) Ltd. 110 Cheltenham Rd. Bristol BS6 5RW.

Copyright: ©Bristol Broadsides and the authors (1983)

Cover design by: Hazel Gower.

Edited by: Ian Bild

Printed and
typeset by: Fingerprints Community Litho (TU), Cardiff. FP.242

ISBN 0 906944 10 4 (paperback)
ISBN 0 906944 16 3 (hardback)

Bristol Broadsides is a member group of the Federation of Worker Writers' and Community Publishers.

The authors and publishers would like to thank the following for their permission to reproduce illustrations:

Blaise Castle House Museum, Henbury Bristol: Page 69, Page 99, Page 105, Page 108, Page 124
City of Bristol Record Office: Frontcover (ref. 11172 (11)), Page 17 (ref. 11172 (11)), Page 74 (ref. 27161), Page 79 (ref. 27161), Page 80 (ref. 27161), Page 85 (ref. 32080/TC4/16/1), Page 139 (ref. 11169 (1)), Page 152 (ref. 12452 (5)).
Chief Environmental Health Officer (Bristol): Page 7, Page 13, Page 22, Page 27, Page 30, Page 131, Page 134, Page 137, Page 145, Page 147.
Mrs Hall: Page 35.
Port of Bristol Authority: Page 72, Page 76, Page 82, Page 89, Page 91, Page 94

CONTENTS

Radical Childhood (1889-1939)

- Stephen Humphries.   5

The Bristol Socialist Society, and John Wall
the shoemaker poet (1885 - 1914)

- Sally Mullen   36

Trade Unionism in Bristol (1910-1926)

- Bob Whitfield   68

Bristol Women in Action (1839-1919)

- Ellen Malos.   97

People's Housing in Bristol (1870-1939)

- Madge Dresser.   129

INTRODUCTION

Who were Bristol's shoemaker poets?
Who burnt the Suffragettes' shop in Queens Rd and why?
Why did people give the landlord the 'bump' or 'put 'im in the Promised Land'?
What was Bristol's Black Friday?
Who were the Monkey Town Mob and the Black Hand Gang?

You will find the answers to these and many other questions in this book on *Bristol's Other History*. It is a history which has largely been ignored but which forms a vital part of the city's past.

Bristol's Other History begins to delve into our radical heritage. The book cannot be a comprehensive account of Bristol's radical history, but it looks at five important areas: Women's Movements (1839 - 1919) ,Trade Unionism (1910 - 1926), People's Housing (1870 - 1939), Radical Childhood (1889 - 1939) and Socialist activities and the Shoemaker poets (1885 - 1914).

For a city that supposedly has little or no radical tradition, so much material has come to light. This book is the first in a series which will try to cover most of the important topics. In future titles we have planned to look at: the Bristol coal miners and their union, unemployed struggles, Socialist Sunday Schools, Women in the Labour Movement and much else.

Bristol Broadsides - a non-profit making publishing co-op - has produced this book, which is an important extension to the work it has already done. Previous publications which include such titles as *Bristol as We remember it, Toby* (the story of a local tramp), *Arthur and Me* and *Shush Mum's Writing* have concentrated on people's history and creative writing. Our aims are to begin democratising history and culture and to provide access to print for 'ordinary' people.

Bristol's Other History includes researched material in combination with oral history. We see this book as complementary to the others we have published. It looks at the lives not of the rich and powerful but of working people, and looks at some of the ways in which people have organised to improve conditions and to struggle for a better society in which to live.

Ian Bild.

BATH COLLEGE OF HIGHER EDUCATION NEWTON PARK LIBRARY

DISCARD

CLASS No. 942. 41 BRI

ACC No. 836516

Radical Childhood in Bristol 1889 - 1939

Stephen Humphries

Classroom disobedience, dis-affection from school work, school strikes, street gang violence, larking about, rebellious sexual behaviour and social crime are some of the topics discussed in this article. It explores a much neglected area of radical history - the day to day struggle to win space from oppressive and exploitative institutions. It will focus upon the everyday resistance of working-class children and youth to authority during the period 1889 to 1939.

Since adults, normally middle-class adults, have in the past controlled most printed sources of evidence, these have consistently presented a hostile and distorted view of the resistance of working-class youth. For example, most school punishment books, press reports and police records of the period condemn all forms of rebellious behaviour committed by young people in a torrent of abusive language. In order to penetrate beneath these accusations of ignorance and immorality, and to discover the real motives and meanings that triggered rebellious behaviour, I have used the memories of old working-class Bristolians, some of whom stand accused in the official records of acts of resistance to authority.[1] In using oral history it has been possible to rescue some of the traditions of resistance of young people, which were of fundamental importance in their material and psychological struggle for survival.

Truancy

The development of a compulsory elementary education system for working-class children was viewed as a means of training young minds to fit into the existing class structure by impressing values of obedience, punctuality, regularity, patriotism, hard work, competitive individualism, and so on.[2]

Although the school attendance rate in Bristol rose steadily from approximately 60 per cent in the 1880s to over 85 per cent by the 1900s, this increase was achieved more by coercion than by consent, and the school authorities were unable to weed out truancy altogether.[3]

It is possible to identify three different types of truancy.[4] First there was an occasional and opportunist form of resistance practised by many working-class children which involved absconding from school several times each year to play in the fields, go to fairs, markets and the dockside, and later to swimming baths and picture palaces. One common ploy amongst children attending schools in central Bristol was to 'mooch off' to picnic and play on Brandon Hill, as Rose Gardner, recalling her Castle Green schooldays in the 1900s, remembers.

> *We hated school my sisters and I so we'd mooch off some afternoons, get a bottle of water and a bit of bread and marg from home, then go over Brandon Hill and have a picnic and play on the cannons. We thought that was marvellous.*(5)

In the early part of the century there were many open fields, streams and ponds on the fringes of the city which together formed a tantalising playground that lured many children away from their lessons. Tom Smith, for example, recalled truanting from Newfoundland Road school to catch 'tiddlers' on spring and summer afternoons in the pre-First World War period.

> *I might go up on Purdown and play games up there. Or there was a little stream not far from us which had tadpoles in and tiddlers - young fish - in. We'd take a jam jar and catch some of those.*(6)

In contrast to occasional and spontaneous absence, there was secondly incessant often long term truancy, deriving from a profound aversion to various aspects of school. Some of the most important motives influencing this type of truancy were a desire for independence and adventure, fear of a particular teacher or lesson, victimisation due to poverty, or difficulties with learning as a consequence of poor health, especially defective eyesight or hearing. Charlie Holbrooke, a docker's son born in Redcliffe in 1890, felt compelled to escape from the regimented school routine in order to experience the freedom, independence and excitement of life on the city streets. Although he was expelled from a number of schools for his persistent truancy and defiance in the classroom, he became so practised in the art of swimming that he was schoolboy swimming champion in Bristol at the age of ten.

> *I didn't like school - I used to go on the knock three or four times a week. I used to go down the baths swimming 'cos I was very fond of swimming - they couldn't keep me out of the swimming pool... My mother had to hide me trousers away from me. If she didn't hide me trousers away from me I used to go down the station, Temple Meads station, carrying parcels and that to get a few coppers for mother, like.*(7)

In the third type of truancy, non-attendance at school was essentially determined by poverty and social deprivation. The necessity of children to take part-time or full-time employment to supplement the family income, and the need to assist overworked mothers with domestic chores and child-minding duties, were both characteristic features. Although this type of truancy often involved the collaboration of parents, on some occasions hungry

Children posing for the photographer on the steps of Palmers Cottage, Stillhouse Lane. (The building was demolished in the 1920s).

children would take the initiative and arrange jobs during school hours, buying meals with the proceeds, as Bill Woods, recalling his St Philips childhood in the early part of the century, remembers.

> *When I was a boy getting on for twelve, thirteen or fourteen, they used to have what they call the cattle market. And every Thursday afternoon I was always missing from school, I used to go on the mooch. And there was a man by the name of Moxham, he was in charge of the farmer's cows, and he used to split them up into different sorts, for selling. And you used to have to stand there in between the two lots to stop them from mixing in with one another. And by the time you was finished you would get something or other off this fellow for looking after the cows. [With another boy], we'd work it between us that one of us would look after the other's cows while the other went over and had a ha'peth of stew in Lloyds' coffee shop in Feeder Road.*(8)

In the classroom

However the most persistent opposition of children to compulsory schooling occured in the classroom itself. Their enforced confinement in institutions which had little to offer apart from rote learning, rigid discipline manners and morals which were often alien and meaningless, led to a constantly antagonistic atmosphere. Most commonly the pupil's resistance was experienced in acts of disobedience, disorderly conduct and a reluctant and apathetic attitude towards learning. This non-cooperative and sometimes openly hostile behaviour, together with the large size of classes and the inadequately trained or equipped teachers, combined to produce a potentially dangerous conflict situation. Elementary schools attempted to resolve this conflict by tightly regulating the learning environment and by resorting to the traditional authoritarian methods of fear and punishment. In addition to the canings which remained a common occurrence in many Bristol schools throughout the period 1889 to 1939, some teachers devised sadistic tortures to control disobedient children, as Elsie Morris, who attended St Gabriel's School in Easton in the early part of the century, remembers.

> *In the school hall we had a clock in the middle. And I was a chatterbox, and if you were caught talking by the headmistress, she had a red flannel 'tongue' and she used to tie it round behind your ears with a piece of tape, and you had to stand under the clock for an hour with your hands on the top of your head.*(9)

Many working class children and their parents refused to submit passively to this punitive treatment. Young children often placed a hair across the palm of the their hand, believing in its magical power to break the cane on impact, or rubbed resin into their hands to toughen the skin and immunise them from the pain. The protection offered by such strategies was more often mythical than real. Older children, however, were occasionally successful in hiding, stealing or burning the teacher's cane, as Ron Tucker, recalling his schooldays at Charborough Road, Filton, in the 1930s, remembers.

> *Some of the teachers weren't exactly God's gift to education. Some of them were a bit free and easy with the cane. There was one bloke, an ex-boxer, Mr Simpson, he could be a bugger. If you weren't concentrating he'd jab you with his fingers on the side of your head or in your stomach. Now I didn't go in for any heroics myself, but one morning I heard a whisper what had happened. Three or four other boys thought there was a bit of injustice about this caning, so they'd got rid of the canes. They must have said, 'Right, we'll make it difficult for them, they can't use the cane if it's not there'. What they did, they hid some of the canes in the girders in the classroom (God knows how they got up there - they must have swung like monkeys). And they never got those canes down. And another cane they shoved in the big stove that heated the school. There was a big hoo-hah about it but they never caught anybody.*(10)

Children and parents sometimes resorted to physical force in order to resist the excesses of school staff. Older boys and girls would seek immediate revenge on brutal and unpopular teachers by throwing ink pots, kicking or punching them. Sometimes children would refuse to accept the caning ritual passively and would attempt to snatch the cane from the teacher's grasp, or would protect friends from punishment by attacking the teacher. Some working-class parents refused to acknowledge the teacher's right to punish their children physically for disobedience, and angry mothers and fathers would sometimes enter the classroom and threaten a teacher with violence should the canings continue. Although parents were often most protective towards a daughter, they were occasionally provoked into bitter protests and threats by the unfair and brutal caning of a son, as Tom Smith recalls.

> *Painting and drawing I was an absolute dud at. And one day we were given some drawing to do, we had to draw a piece of fruit, I think it was an apple an' I made such a hopeless mess of it that he made me do it again. And I did it again about half a dozen times, and still they weren't satisfied, and I had the cane because they said I wasn't trying. So it gave me a bad weal on my hand. 'Course my Dad saw it when I got home. He said, 'Where did you get that from? Why did you have the cane?' So I told him and he said, 'I'll come round and see your teacher'. The teacher was a real bully, so Dad, well, he threatened that he'd do him*

personally if he did anything like that again.

If an individual teacher used particularly savage punishments which endangered the physical health and safety of the pupils, some concerned parents would remove their children and place them in an alternative school, as Charlie Hopwood, recalling his childhood in the Castle Green neighbourhood in the 1920s, remembers.

> *My mother took us away from a certain school in Bristol because the headmaster of that particular school used to have a little 'tiddly', and he used to get a bit tipsy, and he was always punishing the boys. And he punished my brother one day by hitting him on the head with a book and he was ill afterwards, he had a sort of paralysis down one side of his face, and that was the only time I've known my mother come to the school and create. And she marched us off, the two of us twins, and my other two brothers were marched away, and we were taken to another school.*(11)

The insistence on rigid discipline and the regular resort to corporal punishment in many schools was often counter-productive in its effects, for, instead of cultivating obedience and submission to authority, it sometimes planted seeds of injustice, resentment and resistance in young minds. May Loveridge, for example, recalls how the cold, formal manner and the sadistic infliction of punishments by some of the nuns who taught at St Nicholas of Tolentine School in the 1920s, led her to reject the Roman Catholic faith.

> *The teachers that were nuns, they were, excuse me, buggers... There seemed to be a cruelness or something. Too strict, they weren't human, like you couldn't go and speak to them or tell them anything or confide in them or anything, they were too stern... Once the priest saw two children talking in the back row and he threw a bible right through the church at them... I mean they were strict, disciplined themselves, weren't they? I suppose they were the same way with the kids but, ooh, they would wrap you over the knuckles with a ruler, gor! You'd see the expression on their face when they do it as though they were delighted in doing it, some of them. Well, as soon as I was fourteen I turned right from religion, never gone in a Roman Catholic church since I was fourteen, soon as I left school.*(12)

School Strikes

The underlying tension and antagonism between children and the school authorities occasionally exploded into acts of collective resistance such as the school strikes which occurred in the city in October 1889, September 1911 and October 1914. In 1889 and 1911 children in some Bristol schools followed the militant strike action of elementary school pupils in over sixty major towns in Britain, who disrupted the school routine by parading in the streets, demanding shorter school terms and school hours, and the abolition of corporal punishment and homework.(13) These strikes collapsed after only a few hours or at most a few days, as a result of the coercive action of a combination of schoolteachers, attendance officers and policemen. In October 1914 a strike was organised at St Jude's School, protesting against the exploitation of monitors and demanding payment for menial duties. However, the strike was crushed before the children could attract support from pupils in other local schools. Charlie Dallimore remembers how it was repressed with such brutality that even his own severely disciplinarian father was shocked by the inhumanity of the punishments.

Sam Brick, he was the ringleader... He was a quiet chap, must have had trade unionism in his blood, got it from his father I suppose. Well, it was a Friday, we was talking in the playground: 'We ought to go out on strike, threepence a week for monitors, we ain't doing this for nothing, and half a day Wednesdays. Well, in them days they used to carry news placards - magic - find some of them. We turned them over and done writing on them. We agreed that when the Monday morning came and we'll strike. Well, we was all outside the school on strike - it was mostly the older ones - I should say up to about a hundred of us. We then chased along to Hannah More School, we climbed up there calling the kids to come out, like, 'We're on strike'. Anyhow, the teachers started chasing us away, so we chased from there up to St Barnabas, and they was all out in the playground, we got a couple of them to climb over but that's all. It got round in the morning, the School Board and the Minister of St Jude's had gone round to tell the parents that the children's on strike, and as soon as I had me dinner me mother said, 'Come on back, you, come.' And when I were going down the street there were other kids coming along where they had got hold of them. 'Course they was threatened with summonses. The school belonged to the church at that time, St Jude's Church, and they had a curate there, a great big strapping chap, Higgins his name was... The next morning there was Higgins stood in there, and the vicar. So the vicar gave a lecture about this striking business, how wicked we was and everything else, and, 'Course you can't go unpunished for a thing like that'. So he read out Sam Brick was the ringleader. 'Come out Sam Brick'. He walks out and he was a big chap. Along comes this Mr Higgins, he had a cane, he was a beauty, oh he was a proper one, and wallop, he had three on each hand. Now Sam Brick fainted on his last one - you could tell how he laid it in. They brought him round and sat him back. I come out in the next group, two on each hand. He'd catch you across the wrist and it swelled up immediately. Anyhow, my brother was in the next group, and when our Robert went up Higgins looked at him and says, 'Did your Charlie take you out? Did you want to go?' 'Course, our Robert says, 'No! I didn't want to go out, 'twas our Charlie, he made me go out'. 'Oh, did he? You go and sit down. Charlie Dallimore, come out again.' I had another one on each hand. I went home. Now my father was a genuine bloke. Now when he heard all about it he started undoing the buckle of his belt, 'cos that's what you had in them days - the buckle on you. I said, 'Oh God, don't hit me, Dad', I said, 'I've had enough'. He said, 'What do you mean? You haven't had enough by far. They ought to have taken thee down and birched thee'. I said, 'Look at my arms', and he looked at it - me hands and me arms all swelled up. He said, 'My God, I'd like to have him here now, and I'd put the buckle into him'. He said, 'That's cruel'.(14)

The Street

Just as in the educational sphere schools were involved in an ideological process of character formation and control of working-class children, so in the leisure sphere many voluntary and statutory organisations that emerged during our period shared similar repressive aims. The uniformed youth movements such as the Boy Scouts, the Girl Guides and the Boys Brigades, and the church sponsored Girl's Friendly Societies, were all concerned with shaping the character of working-class youth into a conservative, conformist and disciplined mould. The problem they all shared was how best to tame the informal and independent street culture of young people and to exert adult supervision and control over their leisure activities during the impressionable adolescent years. Each organisation adopted varying methods to attract working-class youth into its ranks, the Boy's Brigades stressing discipline, drill and mock military manoeuvres, the Boy Scouts combining the appeal of patriotism, militarism and back-to-nature romanticism, and the Girl's Friendly Societies offering training in domestic duties and skills.(15)

Although all these organisations boasted impressive recruitment figures, interviews with old people suggest that they met with only limited success in changing the way their members behaved. The resilient and rebellious traditions of the street were often stronger. Of these traditions, the most important source of resistance was street-gang membership, which offered an alternative form of leisure-time activity and an alternative form of attitudes and values. Most Bristolian working-class boys and some girls drifted in and out of semi-delinquent, loosely-structured street gangs between the ages of ten and eighteen. These informal gangs were often defined more in opposition to rival

Children playing in Great George Street, St. Judes, 1936 on a site where houses had been demolished by the Bristol Corporation.

streets than in terms of any distinctive internal identity, and essentially originated in the overcrowding of families in densely-packed neighbourhoods in which the street was the only available play and leisure space for the young. The names that they adopted such as the Monkey Town Mob of St Philips or the Bloy Street Gang of Easton were often based on the neighbourhood or the street where the members lived.

The principal concern of young members was to transcend their inferior class position and their experience of poverty and inequality by asserting a proud and rebellious group indentity. The semi-delinquent image projected by many street gangs was shaped by three main characteristics: an assertion of masculinity, a desire to create action and excitement out of the monotonous daily routine, and an exploitation of any opportunity to supplement their meagre diet and income. These focal concerns often led street gangs to create conflict situations in which excitement or material gain could be achieved and machismo proved. Often the most rewarding and challenging situations were those which involved law breaking and violent behaviour. Such activities took several interrelated forms - territorial battles, vandalism, petty crime and conflicts with the police.

Territorial battles were rooted in fierce rivalries between local neighbourhood gangs and such conflicts were commonplace in most working-class districts of Bristol throughout our period. Bill Woods remembers belonging to the infamous St Philips Monkey Town mob in the early part of the century.

> *We had a mob, the Monkey Town Mob we was called. And we used to, with stones and ash buckets or ash bin covers, or whatever we could catch hold of, we used to go and charge Barton Hill, throwing stones at one another. After school, twenty or perhaps thirty, all according to where it was, you'd charge Barton Hill, then you'd go over and charge Brislington, then we'd charge the Dings...If we, say, live round Chapel Street or Barsden Street or Stanhope street, anywhere round there, we'd turn round and say, 'Here, we'll go an' charge Barton Hill tonight'. Go down the Common, then go all round the street shouting to the boys, 'Come on'.*

The main weapons used by opposing gangs were sticks and stones as is illustrated by Fred Coles's recollections of street-gang conflicts in Easton during the pre-First World War period.

> *I can remember when Saffron Street declared war on Bloy Street. And I can see the fighting now, and I can remember one chap - he was on a bike - and someone put a stick in there and all of the spikes came out of his wheel. And then, another time I can remember, John Street, they came*

round for a fight. We had enough timber left over after to build a shed.(16)

In the St Judes area, notorious for its poverty, deprivation and violence, gangs of older boys would carry more dangerous weapons like the improvised 'blood knot', remembered by Charlie Dallimore.

We used to get a piece of iron, a bolt a iron bolt and get a piece of rope, wrap that all the way round and he did hang and we used to swing 'e. 'Course, windows did get broken. And that was called a blood knot.

However, dangerous weapons were possessed by only a small minority of Bristol gangs and, even then, they were rarely used and were carried more as symbols of resistance to respectable society. And although territorial conflicts between rival gangs were often seen by middle-class commentators as evidence of an ignorant and immoral culture, interviews show that they were to a large extent ritualised and involved customary constraints which prevented serious injury. Gangs usually directed their hostility towards opponents of a similar age and dispositon, rarely victimising innocent bystanders. Many conflicts did not progress beyond the preliminary rituals of eye contact, verbal abuse and pushing and shoving. Violent feuds between neighbourhoods were often restricted to annual affairs. And, in face-to-face confrontations, most boys used their fists rather than the sticks and belts that they carried, as few of them wished to risk serious injury to themselves or others. Sometimes disputes would be settled by one from either side, fighting on behalf of his gang. Tom Smith, for example, remembers how a potentially violent confrontation between rival Bristol gangs at Weston in the early part of the century was averted by a combat between individual gang members that was governed by a strict code of honour.

There was gangs. Oh yes, this street would take on the next street and fight. They'd fight just because they had happened to meet and start calling them names to one another. And of course one would hit another about calling him a name he didn't like. Then of course somebody else would join in. I always remember one fellow that was in a crowd I was in, we always thought him a bit of a boob. But we were down Weston-Super-Mare and one from each side started arguing, and he went up to the other fellow that was in our gang and said, 'Come on, leave this to me'. And we never dreamt for one moment at the time, but ye Gods, could he box! He gave the other fellow a darn right hammering. But there was a sort of code of honour. If there were two fellows fighting, one from each side, they fought on behalf of the crowd. There was no interference.

Petty crime was another activity occasionally practised by juvenile street gangs. It is important to remember the meagre diet, the inadequate clothing and the poor health experienced by many working class children, all of which made material and physical deprivation a powerful motive for theft. Most gang thefts took place in shops, and if money was stolen as opposed to food it was quite quickly spent on a feast for those involved in the crime. However, if detected and arrested, gang members faced a battery of severe punitive measures which ranged between a fine, a flogging, committal to an Industrial School, a Reformatory or borstal, or a sentence in a local workhouse or prison. Henry Teague, a street gang leader in Bedminster in the 1890s, received a more lenient sentence than most for his part in a gang raid on a local hardware shop.

> *I was eleven at the time... There was a gang of four or five of us went into a hardware shop and we emptied his till. And we went to a little coffee shop and bought cakes and tea. And we wasn't satisfied with that, so we made a second visit to the hardware shop and we got caught. On the first occasion the proprietor was behind his glass door reading his newspaper and we did it so quietly that he didn't detect us, but he caught us on the second visit and we was remanded at Stapleton Workhouse for a week... We picked oakum - it's like a tar rope - and we had to unravel it for some purpose or another. And they put an old pauper in charge of us, and mind you gave us plenty of wallopings during the week that we was in there. And we was put in a room with a high wall and we couldn't see anything with this high wall right around us... And at the end of the week we was let off in court - we were let off with a caution and a fine of four shillings.*(17)

Street gang members either operating in groups or as individuals, also possessed many devious strategies for gaining illegal free entry to cinemas, music halls and sporting events. Fred Lacock, for example, remembers how his lack of pocket money never prevented him from attending Bristol Rovers matches on Saturday afternoons in the early part of the century.

> *I used to watch Bristol Rovers play, but I didn't pay, not then... I used to go round to Eastville Park, under the arches, across the river, and up over the boards.*(18)

Territorial battles and petty crime brought street gangs into bitter conflict with the police. This hostility was further aggravated by the enforcement by the police, of elaborate rules and regulations designed to prevent and prosecute any young people who indulged in 'dangerous play' such as football, gambling or chasing games in the street. Although these regulations were justified as a necessary precaution for the protection of life, property and the smooth flow of

Group of children and adults in Waters Place, Bedminster (Date not known).

traffic, there is much evidence to suggest that the police, in response to the moral crusades of middle-class reformers for the elimination of street activities, were often petty and brutal in their treatment of those who resisted the law. Incidents in which gang members would challenge or threaten policemen were fairly common. The police responded with a policy of immediate retribution in the street, which usually involved punching, kicking or flicking offenders with their capes.(19) Prosecutions tended to be reserved for young people who persistently opposed the law. This indiscriminate and summary punishment of offenders often resulted in the victimisation of innocent children, which in turn reinforced hostility towards the police, as Henry Teague, recalling an incident that occured in Bedminster in the 1890s, remembers.

I had the biggest belting off a policeman that I can ever remember. I was innocent, quite innocent, I didn't deserve it - if I had I wouldn't have minded. When I was a boy I had a pal in the next street and we was both magic lantern mad. And George said to me, George Betty his name was, he said "Ere Jack, come round to our house tonight to see my magic'. We both had magic lanterns. I said, 'Yes, I will'. So I went round and we had a lovely evening together watching his slides. Then his mum came in and said, 'Come on Johnny, you better be going off now, 'tis nigh nine o' clock, your mother will be wondering where you are'. Well I left and George said, 'I'll come as far as home with you, Jack'. I lived in a court, Union Court, right down opposite Bedminster Bridge Board School - and as we approached home, there was a gang of chaps rushed in front of us and a policeman after them. So George said to me, he said, 'Better not turn in, Jack. We better run along with them or else he'll think that we were with that mob'. I turned round to him and said, 'No, don't wanna worry, we haven't been doing any harm'. So we turned indoors and only about a minute after a knock came at the door. I opened the door and there was a policeman. He said, 'Hello Guvnor, I gotcha then, haven't I?' And I was a saucey little devil then mind, I said, What do you mean, got me? I haven't been doing no harm'. He said, 'You was with that mob'. I said, 'I wasn't with that mob. I've been round my friend's house all the evening watching a magic lantern'. But he walked straight in. Mother was sat in the fireplace with our latest baby. He took his belt off and he put me over a chair and he flogged me. And I can see his helmet now rolling across the fireplace as it fell off his head... [Mother] made no protest at all. And my father was upstairs, more or less drunk he was. He was up there undisturbed - I don't think he heard it. But of course if he'd had a mind he'd have given him policeman. Well, after he give me a flogging, he said, 'Now I'll summons you', but I didn't hear any more after that...But I was absolutely innocent of anything that night. I didn't deserve it but he didn't believe me.

In gangs in which the members shared left-wing political sympathies, opposition to the police and to other authority figures took on a more subversive significance. One such gang was the Bedminster Black Hand Gang, which Mike Osborne belonged to in the 1920s.

I got my introduction by a few words about Socialism. They knew I was left-wing and strong and the Black Hand Gang was supposed to be a throwback to the Anarchists. [The initiation ceremony] was cutting my brother's wrists so the blood would run into another... The gang wanted to bring home trophies and what we'd do, three together, it was very risky doing it! knock a copper's helmet off, and then whip his helmet, and we got away with it... We were what you call gallants, gallants we were... One day we went across the fields and there was a hunting party. party. They were out hunting and they had an autocratic gentleman in a red coat, a face the colour of his coat. He asked me if I could open the gate for'n and I refused. I said, 'I don't approve of your bloodthirsty sport'. And he threatened to put the crop over me, across me neck. I shook 'im off his horse, I caught hold of'n, and tried to throw 'im in the brook, and if I'd had any assistance come this way I'd have done so. We had to go to the magistrates. 'Twas an harmless prank, but these people didn't think so.(20)

Although the street gang did provide a space for working-class youth, free from the authoritarian control and ideological manipulation of provided leisure organisations, its activities should not be sentimentalised or celebrated. For, despite the fact that gang members adopted an aggressive and rebellious stance against respectable society, this resistance was itself riddled with contradictions. Class feelings of anger and bitterness were often misdirected into divisive intra-class conflict, such as territorial gang rivalry and vandalism. And even when gang resentment crystallised into a more class-conscious form, hostility was frequently aimed at personalised targets such as a policeman, a shopkeeper or a local notable. Thus the enormous energy, solidarity and hostility generated by street gangs was guided away from class conflict into activities which could have little impact on the organisation and control of wider power structures.

Larking about

Another important cultural tradition was larking about, and it was practised in many contexts, for example in the street, at school, at church and at work. It served a variety of purposes: to defeat boredom and fear, to resist authoritarian control and ideological manipulation, to create excitement and adventure, and so on. Interviews suggest that during our period there was an increase in larking about, produced by the creative clash between the independent traditions of working-class youth culture and the extensive statutory and voluntary attempts to regulate it.

In the streets of Bristol, the favourite form of larking about was the practical joke, which aimed at irritating and infuriating adults. Working-class children possessed a huge repertoire of such jokes, the most common of which was the illegal game of door knocking and bell ringing known as 'knock out Ginger', and the filling of sugar bags with horse dung, which were dropped on pavements in the hope that they would be picked up and carried home by unsuspecting mothers. And, as Tom Radway recalling his childhood in St Judes in the 1900s remembers, there would be a rapid turnover of playful pranks in every neighbourhood, for many jokes became redundant as soon as they were common knowledge in the area.

> *You couldn't do it too often 'cos your neighbours'd twig it. But another game we got away with for a time was to put a kiddy in a sack on the pavement and wait for an old lady to come, and you'd say, 'Give me a hand missus to pick this bag of coal up', and as she went to lift the bag up, you kicked, see, and she'd start screaming and you got out of the bag and away you went.*(21)

In school there were a number of different forms of larking about which provided comic relief from the monotonous daily routine. Ada Iles' recollection of the larking about of Two Mile Hill school pupils in the early part of the century vividly illustrates the wide range of disruptive tactics, such as parody singing, mimicry and sabotage, that children employed to gain revenge on authority figures. Her memories also illuminate the way in which children, through a combination of individual deviousness and fierce group solidarity, were able to ensure that on most occasions their insulting jokes and sabotage tactics remained undetected and unpunished.

> *There was a lot of larking about went on at Two Mile Hill. In assembly, when we were singing a hymn like Abide With Me, a few of us'd put in a few funny words we all knew beforehand. Then the teacher'd ring her bell - 'Who done it?' - and they'd never find out, so sometimes we'd all forfeit our play... One of the teachers was in the Salvation Army and we'd a call out, 'She's the Sally Army, she's safe from sin, she'll go to 'eaven in a comed beef tin'. If they caught you for that you'd a-be punished heavily... And in class, when some was bored, 'twasn't no good for the others to study - they'd tip the inkwell over someone that was studying. 'Please miss, I've 'ad an accident, I've spilt my inkwell over*

such and such'. The teacher couldn't say they done it deliberate and the lesson'd be postponed while they got the cloth and the blotting paper to mop it up... Another thing that was done deliberate to stop the lessons was letting off stink bombs. After a couple of minutes you'd start to smell it and it'd stink the place out. Lessons had to be stopped, all the windows had to be opened, and we did go out into the hall, the smell was so bad. The teacher hardly ever found out who did it because nobody'd tell. We really enjoyed it. We didn't mind the smell 'cos we didn't have no lessons... When our teacher was writing on the blackboard or looking in her book, we'd start taking the mickey, taking her to pieces you might say, but only under our breath. Miss Dugdale her name was, and her nickname was Miss Hoppydehop, because she did have high heeled winklepickers and did walk just so, you know. She was posh, a bit of a snob, and we did insult here wicked behind her back. We made fun of her clothes because they were very severe, tailored clothes, always in drab, dark colours that we didn't like. When she went out of the classroom we'd a-start writing and drawing things on the blackboard, making fun of 'er, saying how ugly and fat she was like. But when we heard her coming back, we'd a-rub it all off, we was so frightened. Once a girl didn't have time to rub it off and the teacher went mad, and went round to every child individually to find out who done it, and everyone said, 'I don't know, I don't know, I don't know'. Then one kid grassed. That kid's life wasn't worth living for the next couple of months. Her mother had to bring and fetch her home from school every day, and she couldn't even go out to play, because all we kids was waiting to grab hold of her.(22)

Disruptive larking about was also a constant problem at Sunday school, chapel and church, which most working-class children were compelled by parents to attend regularly until they began work. Some Bristolian children turned church attendance to their advantage by spending the money entrusted to them by parents for the church collection on sweets or cigarettes, and then faked a contribution during the collection. And interviews reveal that hungry and disenchanted children showed no quarter to the feelings of church workers unable to control them, for during services the more devious children would literally be straining every faculty to sabotage the sacred atmosphere. All these aspects of resistance to religious provision, which increasingly came to be viewed by many older children as irrelevant, manipulative or hypocritical are illustrated in Bert Mullen's recollections of larking about in the early 1930s.

We used to lark around so much in Sunday school that once the bloke that was teaching us started crying. He was telling us how we ought to be well behaved and us little buggers weren't taking any notice of him - we

'The Dings' in St Philips was one of Bristol's most notorious slum areas between the wars. This photo of 42 Union Rd 1919 shows collapsed roof of a house that was apparently still inhabited.

were just messing around, prodding each other and eating sweets. And when he started crying we just laughed even more... For the evening service the old lady'd give me something for the collection, but on the way me and me mates would spend it all on sweets. Instead of listening to the bloody sermon, we'd be sucking sherbert bon bons and larking around. Then when the collection plate came round, us boys would dip our hand in, rattle the coins around a bit, and pass it onto the next person...At one point in the service there'd be this deathly silence when everybody would be feeling holier than thou. Old Gerry Hunter would do his best to save up a big fart for this moment, and he'd let rip a real rumbler. Gerry would look round, and we'd all look round, pretending to be concerned as to where the noise came from. When we got outside we'd kill ourselves laughing. The perfect end to a religious day.(23)

Just as larking about in the street, in school and in church, generated excitement and created space from authoritarian demands and restrictions, so similarly, in the work situation, it helped to reduce frustration and to assert informal control over repetitive and depersonalised production processes. 'Larking' and 'kidding' formed a basic part of the shop floor culture, especially amongst the young. Its most characteristic features were aggressive repartee, practical jokes, illicit smoking and drinking, and raucous singing and horseplay. However, larking about at work could be a hazardous affair, for young workers who were unfortunate enough to be detected were often threatened with dismissal or humiliated by their employers, as Winnie Vickers, recalling her exploits in a Bristol sack factory in the early part of the century, remembers.

I worked in a sack factory, darning coal sacks. And of course the sack factory we worked in created rats, and very often we would see one running about. But my nephew had a toy one, a rubber one, and I took 'n to work one afternoon, and the person that worked next to me, I hid it under her pile of sacks. And of course, just as she saw it, it happened to be the boss come round, and she screamed out, and when he come over, he could see it was a rubber rat. So he said, 'Will the person who put the rat there own up?' So I said, 'Yes, it was me'. He said, 'I guessed as much, up to the office'. And he gave me a ticking off, and he said, 'I think you'll have to have your cards on Saturday and finish up'. So I said, 'Well all right'. So on the Saturday all the wages were paid out to the other girls and mine wasn't there. So I said to our forewoman, 'What about my wages?' She said 'You'd better go up and see the boss'. So up I went. I knocked on the door, and he said, 'Come in, please'. I said, 'Can I 'ave my wages and cards please?' So he said, 'Yes, I am sorry that this has happened', and he burst out laughing. So I said, 'I can't see

23

any joke in being out of work. What am I going to do Mister Downey?'
So he said, 'Well, you're not the only one who can play jokes - I can play
jokes as well. I didn't mean to stop you from working'. And I said,
'Thank God!' (24)

The final area in which the practice of larking about acted as a powerful source of resistance to adult control was that of informal relationships between boys and girls. The sexual behaviour of youth was a perennial cause for concern, especially during the late-Victorian and Edwardian period. This anxiety was rooted in the fear that casual relationships between the sexes would damage or destroy the fruits of formal conduct, regularity and obedience, that had been carefully cultivated by various character-forming agencies.(25) Increasingly, the independent courting traditions of working-class youth were subjected to the restrictions imposed by middle-class theories of adolescence, which prescribed a prolonged, regulated and institutionalised dependency on adults as essential to normal and healthy sexual development.(26) The policies of sex segregation generated by these theories were often interpreted and administered in a harsh and punitive manner by lower middle-class officials, especially schoolteachers. These restrictions were reinforced by many working-class parents' imposition of rigid controls on the leisure activities of their children, particularly daughters, in order to avoid the dangers of promiscuity and illegitimacy, and to ensure that they were available to assist with domestic chores at home. However, the authoritarian measures of a combination of schoolteachers, youth workers, employers and parents failed to eliminate a strong undercurrent of resistance to sex suggestion and illicit contact between the sexes, widely referred to as larking about. By the early 1900s the phrase 'larking with the lads' became the watchword for worried officials, denoting the informal friendships which working-class girls persisted in forming with the boys. Young domestic servants, on their occasional days off work, would promenade along Colston Avenue, larking about with the boys, as Bill Hawes remembers.

> *Colston Avenue was known in those days as Skivvies Island... because a lot of the maids from the various houses used to go there, and that's where we spent most of our teenage time. The girls used to walk down one side, the boys used to walk up the other and, toward later in the evening, you could see them pairing off and going off to their various destinations. Most of them went on Brandon Hill, to have a kiss and cuddle - it was quite a game. I think there was many a marriage blossomed from Skivvies Island - it was quite a place for the youngsters to go down and walk up and down, and eyeing girls, whistling and cat-calling, and all that thing.*

Whereas middle-class youth might in their late teens only meet suitable partners through formal introductions, normally by parents, the horseplay and humorous exchanges associated with larking about provided working-class youth with a ritual introduction to anyone they fancied 'getting off' with. Streets and parks provided the main arena for these encounters between the sexes, as Tom Partridge remembers.

> *I used to go with the girls out to the parks... We used to go in little gangs just for the night out. And on a Sunday where they used to do their mixing mostly in Bristol, it was a common thing to spend Sunday evening in town. And what you used to do if you lived on Lawrence Hill, Sunday was a time when you got decked up, dressed up sort of thing, and went out for a walk... Down to Old Market, up Castle Street, possibly on from there on the Downs, and back. And of a weekend, Saturdays and Sundays, Castle Street especially, and Bridge Street, used to be crowded with people, girls, boys - crowded. You'd be amazed, you'd think there was a big match today, but that used to be people just going out for walks... You used to meet different people you hadn't seen before, not from your own district, and then of course you'd get talking and larking around.*(27)

Teenage girls often cultivated a proud and playful promenading image which was designed to be sexually provocative and to attract male admiration and advances. But, at least until the 1920s, most girls who wished to experiment with make-up and dyed hair had to be extremely devious and secretive in their attempts to beautify themselves, in order to avoid adult disapproval and reprimands, as Winnie Davis remembers.

> *Mother wouldn't allow me to use paint or powder or anything like that... I used to get threepenny-worth of peroxide and put it on me hair, then I'd wash it. Then perhaps a neighbour would say, 'Haven't your Winnie got lovely hair?' My mother would say, 'Yes she washed it last night. If she'd only do it more often, she'd keep it that colour'. 'Course, it was this peroxide, but she didn't know... All the girls done it, and I done it. I couldn't do up, so I used to get a rose petal, because you always had flowers in your hat, and I took a rose out and wetted it, just dabbed it on me cheeks, and lipstick on. Perhaps someone would be in the house and they'd say, 'Don't Winnie look warm?'*(28)

Some parents were so fearful of the consequences of 'larking with the lads' that they would sometimes refuse to allow their daughters out, or would insist that they arrive home by eight or nine o'clock in the evening, even though they might be in their late teens or early twenties. This type of parental intolerance and interference sometimes led to intense conflict and resentment within the family, especially when teenage daughters were determined to resist adult control. However, by adopting an intransigent stance, daughters often forced parents reluctantly to acknowledge their independence, as Jessie Niblett, bitterly recalling her experiences of domestic conflict in St Philips in the early part of the century, remembers.

> *I had to be in at nine o'clock at night. I went to bed one night, I went to bed with all me clothes on. I opened the window, got out, went down over the roof in the kitchen, into the garden, over the wall, round the lane, and went in town up by the shops, after the chaps. I came in about eleven o'clock and my father was waiting for me. My sister had given me away. It wasn't the first time I gone to bed with all me clothes on, so he used to look in to see if we was in bed. She'd told him and he was up waiting for me - he was stood in the passage, in the dark. As I went to push the door to go in, I had one each side of my face. I screeched the street down 'cos I didn't know who it was. Then I got a kick - I got a hole here in my back - he kicked me right in the bottom of my spine. I never forgot that... But I dared and went the next night. Aye, I did! I thought, well, I've had the hiding, and that's that... My sister told father I was gone and he just let me go and carry on - he didn't bother with me any more. He thought I'd learnt a lesson. I'd learnt a lesson, but not in the way he thought I'd learnt a lesson.(29)*

Social Crime

Another tradition of resistance was that of social crime, which involved the committing of minor crimes against property. Unlike the crimes committed by street gangs, social crime was often condoned or even initiated by parents and families. Most contemporary commentators condemned this behaviour as an expression of the ignorance, immorality and indiscipline of the working-class family. However, I believe that a number of these offences can more accurately be understood as a form of social crime. They were motivated and justified by the 'social' impetus of struggle for family survival in the face of grinding poverty, as opposed to the 'anti-social' motive of adolescent selfishness imputed by those in authority.(30) It is important to remember that, despite gradual improvements in the standard of living, many working-class Bristolians experienced varying degrees of poverty and deprivation 1889 to 1939. For example, Herbert Tout's major investigation into the standard of living in Bristol in 1937, a year of exceptional prosperity and high employment, revealed that 'there are perhaps 40,000 people in the area living in actual poverty and among them a disproportionate number of children'.(31)

Hotwells, a working class area at least since the early 18th century had many dilapidated buildings by the First World War and was one of the 'pockets' of slum housing in West Bristol. Large families and homework (were the children cutting up wood to sell?) made conditions even more squalid in these old houses.

The most common type of property theft, viewed by many working-class children and their parents as legitimate despite its illegality, was the reappropriation of nature's bounty to supplement the family's food and fuel supply. This type of offence, known as 'simple and petty larceny', constituted the most important category of juvenile crime during the period under study, and essentially comprised taking coal from pitheads, chumps of wood from timber yards, vegetables from farmer's fields, poaching, and so on. It was amongst families whose survival was threatened by low wages, prolonged unemployment or the death of one of the parents, that crimes of this sort were most common.(32)

In coal mining neighbourhoods, of which there were several in the Bristol area, it was common practice for children to 'pick' or 'scrounge' coal from pit heads, slag heaps or coal depots. Also, poor children would follow horse-drawn coal carts around the streets, collecting any lumps of coal that were accidentally spilt, or occasionally pilfering coal from the cart itself. Most children, however, like Charles Portingale who grew up in St Werburghs in the 1930s, were careful and quick-witted enough to avoid arrest.

Over Fox Road used to be a coal yard... We used to have Grade 1, Grade 2 things for coal, anthracite and all this - they used to start separating it. I used to take a sack over on a night time, and there used to be one part there with the bars bent where somebody had bent it purposely to get in there, and I got in there. Been over in the afternoon and had a look to see which was the grades and memorised it, then take a bag and get through the hole, fill me bag up. And I went over one day - I went about ten o'clock at night time - and filled the bag up. And I was just going to come out - now this was the only place because the spike railings was nine or ten feet high - just coming out with the bag when there was a courting couple stood right by the hole, kissin' and cuddlin' and they was cuddlin' till about half-past twelve from ten o'clock. So my mother - she knows where I've gone - she starts getting hysterical, because she thinks I've been caught. I couldn't go till they went. But at least we had a fire.(33)

Other common targets for juvenile theft in Bristol were orchards, which children would raid and begin 'chowding' or 'scrumping' apples, and shops and markets, whose tantalising displays of sweets, fruit and vegetables invited much pilfering from gangs of children. Sometimes hungry children would abscond from school to feast on stolen food, as Dick Cook, reflecting on his education at Ashton Gate School in the early part of the century, recalls.

I had two brothers in the same class [as me], so you could tell how brilliant I was - they was younger than me. Well, they sneaked off at playime. They pinched some oranges - I think they pinched about a dozen - they must have pinched a box full. When it came to, our Alf and our Tom didn't come back, and they sent me to find them. I knew where I'd find them - they'd be down at the waterside scoffing these oranges. I can remember saying, 'You aren't half going to cop it when yous get back'. Our Alf said, 'Never mind about that, get stuck into these oranges'. When they got to school next morning they wanted to know why I didn't come back and I got the pasting instead.(34)

Also, because the countryside was only a short walking distance from any part of the city of Bristol during the period we are looking at, there were many opportunities for poaching available to the urban poor. Occasionally, the survival strategies of working-class families involved conspiratorial collaboration between father and son on poaching expeditions, as Fred Lacock, recalling his Easton childhood in the 1900s, remembers.

My old father, he used to go out Saturday night, come home Sunday morning. He'd have about a dozen rabbits, go out about these woods and trap these rabbits. He used to make his own nets. I used to help him - he would show me how. When the nets were finished with, he'd hide them in the woods. Then he'd tell me where to go and pick them up on a Sunday...He never used to starve, I'll tell you. Neither would I. When I was out of work, after I had a few drinks, I've been up what they called the Black Rocks and steal a bag of spuds out, come home, and been chased by the coppers at night. I wouldn't starve, neither would my old father. He'd get some grub from somewhere.

Poor parents also conspired with their children to deceive the authorities in the infamous 'moonlight flit', to avoid the payment of rent. And some parents were so determined to enjoy an annual family trip to the seaside, apart from those provided for poor children by philanthropic organisations, that they would practice devious tricks in order to avoid paying expensive rail fares that were beyond their means. Iris Bradford, for example, remembers her mother's cunning strategy which aimed at providing free rail travel for her children on the annual family day out to Weston in the late 1920s.

When we went on holiday we never went away for a week, but with the unemployed we used to have a free day out to Weston, and when we got there we had a ticket pinned on us - you know, that our dads were unemployed. But we got a free ride on a fairground and a free stick of rock. That was once a year. Then we'd always go with the Sunday School - because, in those days, the price you paid depended on how many times you went to Sunday School, so we made sure we went every Sunday so that we wouldn't have to pay very much - that was another

*good outing. And then maybe once a year - no more, because my mum
and dad couldn't afford it - they would take us to Weston. And we were
very tiny, all of us, and my mum, what she used to do was to look for the
fattest people coming along the front of the station going into pay.
And then she'd say, 'Now, Iris, you go and stand in between those two
there, and Ivy you go there'. She used to place us in the queue behind
them so she wouldn't have to pay. But I'm sure that the chappie taking
the tickets knew we were there, but they used to turn a blind eye to it. And
you'd never get anybody on the train asking for your ticket, so we did the
same thing at the other end.*(35)

In conclusion, the resistance of working-class children and youth to
authority can broadly be understood in terms of the bitter daily struggle for
survival and control in an essentially exploitative and oppressive environment.
On a material level, the necessity for children to contribute towards the
domestic economy of the working-class family was a key factor that inspired a
number of traditions of resistance, such as social crime and subsistence
truancy. On a psychological level, the struggle to breathe life and spontaneity
into the suffocating daily routine of tedious labour at school and work led to the
development of other traditions of resistance, such as classroom disobedience,
larking about and street-gang membership. Closely related to these struggles
was the attempt of working-class children and youth to assert greater control
over the institutions in which they were incorporated. This was expressed, for
example, in the educational sphere, by truancy, classroom protests against the
worst abuses of authoritarianism and school strikes. Much of this conflict at
school, at work and in leisure time stemmed from a clash between the informal
and independent codes of conduct characteristic of working-class culture, and
the formal, depersonalised and authoritarian nature of official institutions.
Although some of the practices that emerged from this culture were torn with
contradictions or were simply self-destructive, they form part of a creative
cultural tradition that parallels the explicitly political traditions of the working
class in their opposition to class oppression.

Sources for further information

The primary source material available for those who wish to explore the
social history of childhood and youth in Bristol in the past century are of two
types, documentary and oral. The main documentary material comprises the
school log and punishment books held either at the Bristol Public Record
Office or at individual schools, the records held by local organisations such as
the Boys Brigade and the Girl's Friendly Society, press reports and police

records. Occasionally, teachers and officials described the children under their care in vivid detail. Two outstanding examples are the Clifton Parochial School Log Book and the Reports on Pupils contained in the Carlton House Industrial School for Girls, 1875-1900, both held by the Bristol Public Record Office. However, in the majority of cases, accounts of the behaviour of working-class children are restricted to one word or one sentence in length. Even when entries are more extensive, they are usually prescriptive rather than descriptive, often revealing more about the moral preoccupations and prejudices of the middle-class adults who controlled educational and welfare institutions than about the thoughts and feelings of the children contained within them.

A more useful source for reconstructing a recent history of childhood and youth is autobiography. Bristol Broadsides have published a valuable series of individual and collective life histories, *A Bristol Childhood, Bristol as We Remember it, Up Knowle West, Looking Back on Bristol, Arthur and Me,* and *Toby.* There are also a number of interesting unpublished autobiographies of Bristolian working-class childhoods held privately, the most interesting of which are written by Iris Hutchings and Ernest Curme of Bedminster. In addition I have deposited a number of shorter recollections of working-class childhood and youth written by local people in the Avon County Reference Library. I feel certain that an appeal on Radio Bristol or in the local press would bring many more unpublished writings to light.

The richest source materials on the history of working-class childhood and youth are oral interviews. Properly conducted, they can reveal a wealth of detail about family life, schooling, leisure and work experience that has not been recorded in any other form. A useful starting point for anyone wishing to research in this area is the collection of approximately 150 taped interviews deposited by the Bristol People's Oral History Project in the Avon County Reference library, containing memories of childhood and youth of Bristolian working-class men and women born between 1885 and 1925. Also, the Malago Society based at Bedminster Down Comprehensive School have a substantial collection of oral, documentary and photographic material on the history of South Bristol, some of which relates to childhood and youth. Those interested in various aspects of the history of childhood and youth should consider interviewing members of their family, friends and neighbours. The advantage of this approach is that you can frame your own questions and dig for specific information that is relevant to your own particular project. Two basic books on the importance of oral history, interviewing techniques, recording equipment, and so on, are Paul Thompson's *The Voice of the Past* (Oxford 1978) and Stephen Humphries's *Oral History and the Community* (Inter Action - October 1983).

The secondary source material on working-class childhood and youth is rather thin. Although there is a proliferation of histories of the city's public and grammar schools, elementary education has received scant attention. The official histories of secondary schools, the police and youth movements in the area are often hagiographic, focusing upon adult personalities and organisational change, and making only brief and dismissive references to young people. There is a greater abundance of material relating to the post World War 2 period, for example the investigations initiated by the Bristol Social Project into delinquent working-class youth in the area, the bulk of which is contained in John Spencer, *Stress and Release in an Urban Estate* (1964). However, most of this official or semi-official literature tends to view rebellious behaviour in terms of individual inadequacy and neurosis rather than as an expression of deeply-rooted class conflict. I have attempted to redress the balance by situating resistance in the context of class inequality and poverty in my own work on the history of childhood and youth in the city; 'Hurrah For England: Schooling and the Working Class in Bristol 1870-1914', in *Southern History* Vol.1 (1979); Steal to Survive: The Social Crime of Working Class Children 1889-1939', in *Oral History* Vol. 9 no.1 (Spring 1981); and *Hooligans or Rebels? An Oral History of Working Class Childhood and Youth 1889-1939* (Blackwell 1981) - much of the material in this book is drawn from the Bristol collection of tapes.

---

(1) Many of the recollections which appear in this article were collected as part of the 'Bristol People's Oral History Project and I am very grateful to all those who worked on it. Special thanks are due to Pam Scull, Irena Czapska, Jane Dunstan, Kathy Lye, Sally Mullen, Madge Mullen, Tracy Morefield, Linda Vickers, and Anne Oakley for their tape recording and transcribing of many interviews with old people. The project was made possible by the financial and administrative support of the Manpower Services Commission, the Resources for Learning and Development Unit and the Avon County Reference Library in Bristol, and I would like to thank all the staff of these organisations, in particular Ivor Bolt, Philip Waterhouse and Geoff Langley for the advice and assistance they generously gave to us. I am also indebted to all the people we interviewed for their friendly cooperation and to the wardens of many old people's dwellings in Bristol who helped us to arrange most of the interviews. The tapes of all interviews marked 'Bristol collection' in the footnotes can be listened to at the Avon County Reference Library, College Green, Bristol, and form part of the collection of approximately 150 tapes created by the project. The page references after the interview number refer to transcripts which are available for a number of the recordings. Extracts from interviews that I conducted which appear in the text, have not yet been deposited in the library.

(2) See Stephen Humphries, *Hooligans or Rebels? An Oral History of Working Class Childhood and Youth 1889-1939* (Blackwell 1981), especially Chapter 2.

(3) For a more detailed examination of school attendance in Bristol see Stephen Humphries, 'Hurrah for England: Schooling and the Working Class in Bristol 1870-1914', in *Southern History* Vol.1 (1979) pp.171-207.

(4) These different types of truancy are described in more depth in S. Humphries, *Hooligans or Rebels?* op.cit. Chapter 3.

(5) Born 1898, Barton Hill, Bristol. Bus conductress. Father, engine driver. Mother, laundress. Interviewer S. Humphries.

(6) Interview no. 007 p.11 (Bristol collection). Born 1903, Montpelier, Bristol. Journeyman compositor. Father, blacksmith. Mother, housewife. Interviewer, Pam Scull.

(7) Interview no. 032 p.1 (Bristol collection). Born 1890, Redcliffe, Bristol. Army. Father, docker. Mother, pottery worker. Interviewer, Linda Vickers.

(8) Interview no. 005 p.13 (Bristol collection). Born 1902, St Philips Marsh, Bristol. Labourer. Father, engineer. Mother, housewife. Interviewer, Pam Scull.

(9)   Interview no. 049 - written recollections (Bristol collection). Born 1905, Easton, Bristol. Coat maker and tailoress. Father, box maker and messenger for the GPO. Mother, housewife.

(10)   Born Exeter 1927. Technical Clerk. Mother housewife, father printer. Inverviewer S. Humphries.

(11)   Interview no. 064 p.23 (Bristol collection). Born 1915, Castle Green, Bristol. Worker at Bristol Aeroplane Company. Father, merchant seaman. Mother, housewife. Interviewer, Irena Czapska.

(12)   Interview no. 056 p.2 (Bristol collection). Born 1912, Castle Green, Bristol. Domestic servant, waitress, shop assistant. Father army. Mother, housewife. Interviewer, Irena Czapska.

(13)   For more detailed studies of school strikes see S. Humphries *Holigans or Rebels?* op. cit. Chapter 4; Dave Marson, 'Children's Strikes of 1911' (1973); and Pamela Horn, 'The Herefordshire School Strike of 1914' in studies in the local history of Education (History of Education Society 1977)

(14)   Born 1900, St Judes, Bristol. Operative in boot and shoe factory, army service, then lorry driver. Father, operative in boot and shoe factory. Mother, housewife. Interviewer S. Humphries.

(15)   For more detailed studies of the aims and organisation of these youth movements see John Springall, *Youth, Empire and Society* (1977); and David Reeder, 'Predicaments of City Children: Late Victorian and Edwardian Perspectives on Education and Urban Society', pp.75-94, in D. Reeder (ed) *Urban Education in the Nineteenth Century* (1977).

(16)   Interview no. 015 pp.16-18 (Bristol collection). Born 1901, Easton, Bristol. Labourer, store keeper and miner. Father, navy. Mother, housewife and midwife. Interviewer, Pam Scull.

(17)   Interview no. 033 pp.5,6. (Bristol collection). Born 1885, Bedminster, Bristol. Apprentice in printing trade, shop assistant, operative in paint and brush factory, labourer. Father, labourer. Mother, housewife. Interviewer, Kathy Lye.

(18)   Interview no. 009 p.8 (Bristol collection). Born 1899, Easton, Bristol. Machine driller, general labourer. Father, docker. Mother, housewife. Interviewer, Kathy Lye.

(19)   For more detailed historical studies of the antagonistic relationship between working-class youth and police, see S. Humphries. *Hooligans or Rebels?* op. cit. Chapter 7; John Gillis, 'The Evolution of Juvenile Delinquency 1890-1914' in *Past and Present* (May 1975) pp.96-126; and Paul Thompson, *The Edwardians* (1975) pp.67,68.

(20)   Interview no. 067 (Bristol collection). Born 1909, Bedminster, Bristol. Various occupations, became a tramp in his 20s. Father, factory foreman. Mother, housewife and nurse. Interviewer, Tracy Morefield.

(21)   Born 1898, St Judes Bristol. Wheelwright. Father, publican. Mother, housewife. Interviewer, S. Humphries.

(22)   Born 1904, Fishponds, Bristol. Bus conductress. Father, publican. Mother, housewife. Interviewer, S. Humphries.

(23)   Born 1922, Fishponds, Bristol. Telephone salesman. Father, engineer. Mother, forewoman in slipper factory. Interviewer, S. Humphries.

(24)   Interview no. 012 (Bristol collection). Born 1909, Barton Hill, Bristol. Weaver, then darner in sack factory. Father, miner, hod carrier. Mother, cotton spinner. Interviewer, Pam Scull.

(25)   See E.J. Bristow, *Vice and Vigilance: Purity Movements in Britain since 1700* (Dublin 1977); P. Cominos, 'Late Victorian Sexual Respectability' in *International Review of Social History* Vo. VIII (1963) pp.18-48 and Vol. IX (1963) pp.216-250; and S. Humphries, *Hooligans or Rebels?* op. cit. Chapter 5.

(26)   See, John Gillis, *Youth and History* 1974).

(27)   Interview no. 058 pp.24,25. (Bristol collection). Born Cardiff 1911, moved to St George, Bristol, when a child. Hairdresser, then plumber and decorator; afterwards joined army. Father, jobbing builder. Mother, housewife. Interviewer, Irena Czapska.

(28)   Interview no. 002 p.15 (Bristol collection). Born 1899, St Philips, Bristol. Factory operative, then domestic servant. Father, naval engineer, then miner. Mother, housewife. Interviewer, Pam Scull.

(29)   Interview no.001 p.11 (Bristol collection). Born 1896, St Philips, Bristol. Domestic servant, then brewery worker. Father, labourer. Mother, housewife. Interviewer, Jane Dunstan.

(30) For a detailed study of social crime with further references to the illegal activities of children in Bristol, see S. Humphries, 'Steal To Survive; The Social Crime of Working Class Children 1889-1939', in *Oral History* Vol. 9 no.1 (Spring 1981) pp.24.33.

(31) Herbert Tout, *The Standard of Living in Bristol* (1938) p.11.

(32) See, A.M. Carr Sanders, H. Mannheim and E.C. Rhodes, *Young Offenders: An Enquiry into Juvenile D·linquency* (Cambridge 1942); and H. Mannheim, *Social Aspects of Crime Between the Wars* (1940).

(33) Interview no. 059 pp.26,27. (Bristol collection). Born 1921, Baptist Mills, Bristol. Builder's boy, then seaman. Father, bricklayer. Mother, housewife and part-time cleaner. Interviewer, Irena Czapska.

(34) Interview no. 061 p.7 (Bristol collection). Born 1906, Ashton Gate, Bristol. Blacksmith. Father, engineer. Mother, dressmaker and housewife. Interviewer, Kathy Lye.

(35) Born 1921, Bedminster, Bristol. Tobacco factory worker, then shop assistant. Father unemployed for long periods, became postman. Mother, housewife. Interviewer, S. Humphries.

A class of seven year olds from Fonthill Road School, Southmead, taken in 1934.

The Bristol Socialist Society 1885 - 1914
Sally Mullen

The Bristol Socialist Society was formed in 1885 (1). It was one of the most influential and militant socialist groups in the country. (2) Among those who were converted by its activists were Ramsay MacDonald, Ben Tillett and Ernest Bevin. Their socialist faith was a blend of the ethical teachings of William Morris and Edward Carpenter, Marxist ideas of class conflict and non-conformist notions of duty, self-respect and righteousness.

The Bristol Socialist Society successfully fought a number of local battles for freedom of speech and the right to combine; took up unpopular causes of unemployment, sweated labour, bad housing and education; and struggled to convert the working class to the idea of labour representation as a means of improving their lot. In 1891, for example, the City Council attempted to enact bye-laws prohibiting meetings in public parks. The Socialist Society staged protests and together with other Labour and radical groups formed the Right of Public Meetings Committee. This pressure group was eventually successful and established their right to hold meetings in public parks such as Eastville, and Victoria Park, Bedminster. Their struggle to achieve this right, however, met with police interference, which became a regular occurence in nearly all of the labour disputes in Bristol which the Socialist Society supported. The response of one committee representative sums up the spirit of many working class people at this time:

> *There are two or three thousand miners living around one of the parks, and...they will have their meetings. If the Hyde Parks of Bristol are shut against them then down with the railings.* (3)

Whilst the Bristol Socialist Society directly supported the trade unionists in their attempt to unionise workers, especially those in unskilled jobs, they retained a social and cultural identity which was characterised by educational and intellectual development, music, entertainment, outings and rambles, in which their goal of 'brotherhood' could be felt and experienced

In the '80s the Socialist Union met at Elworthy's Coffee Tavern in Bedminster. Such coffee shops were popular meeting places for people of socialist and radical politics. *The Star* and *New Street* were two of the most common, the former being the Trades Council's base, and the latter the place where the Organising Committee regularly met in 1890. This organisation, composed of many socialists and led by the well-known working-class shoemaker poet John Gregory, was committed to the unionisation of unskilled workers, particularly women, and the inculcation of 'Socialist opinions'.

The oldest building where the Bristol Socialists met on a large scale was the

Shepherds' Hall. Socialist discussions and lectures were promoted by the Bristol Sunday Society, founded in 1889, which provided Sunday lectures for working men and women and speakers in the lecture lists included important thinkers such as Prince Kropotkin, George B. Shaw, and Annie Besant. However, whilst the Sunday Society tended towards a more academic, literary and scientific slant, the Bristol Socialist Society lectures were always preceded by a 'good musical programme and followed by discussion'. (4) Possibly it was this extra dimension of activity which distinguished the Socialist Society from other organisations and groups which shared similar ethical aims, such as the Christian Socialist Brotherhood and the Christian Socialists, although of course the two latter groups did not believe in the revolutionary continental tradition of socialism which the Socialist Society embraced.

The open air meetings which took place during the summer months were every Sunday evening at the Downs, and Ashton Park, Bedminster and, during the winter, in the Shepherd's Hall. Lectures and debates also took place every Wednesday at the Socialist Centre in the Horsefair. (5) Mrs Pearce remembers the meetings which the whole family attended at the Hall in 1908 where her father first met socialist and co-operator John Wall the subject of the next section who was also a shoemaker poet.

There was a place called the Shepherd's Hall... There they used to talk over different things...that's where they met... It was a mixed group of people... We used to go there and there used to be my father, my mother, my sister, and myself and we used to go down and watch for Mr and Mrs Wall to come in and my father used to (say), 'Here comes the old school-master and his wife'. So that's how we always thought of him... Well he had that look about him... He had a beard, and he was very genteel in his way...He carried himself like that - he looked stern...yet he was very, very kind.

Clearly these Sunday evenings at the Shepherd's Hall were a family affair and the children frequently participated in the entertainment. Mrs Pearce recalls the pleasure of these meetings:

Oh we used to have some nice times. I can remember they used to have an orchestra and singing and piano playing...they used to have Dolly (John Wall's daughter) and she used to do recitations...and there used to be a violinist, Casey, and he used to play beautiful things...a bird he used to play on the violin and it was really lovely...

In the late 1890s the Socialist Society ran its first Sunday School at the Shepherd's Hall and about eighty children enrolled. This Sunday School ended after four years, and another was set up in the Socialist Centre in the

A gathering of Socialists in the Horsefair including Ben and Mabel Tillet in the centre of the picture & Will Sharland (with the grey beard).

Horsefair where the Society had rented rooms. It is likely that there were many small Socialist Sunday schools which sprang up in different areas, although there is very little documentary evidence relating to them. Oral interviews have uncovered the Cobden Street Socialist Sunday School, situated in the Lawrence Hill district. This school was an informal gathering of the children of local Socialists in a small room where they were taught by ordinary working people the rudiments of socialism. (6) Elder sons and daughters of Socialists frequently ran the Sunday schools, as Mrs Pearce's recollections suggest:

> *Now the Sharlands, the one I took to was Rose Sharland... I was in the school with her... She was a lovely person very, very pretty and tall and she had curly hair and a lovely complexion... She used to come to the Socialist Sunday School where Ethel (John Wall's eldest daughter) used to take me Sunday afternoons. That was in the Haymarket - well, it was just a little shop really, made into a Sunday School, and my husband (John Wall's eldest son) used to teach there and Ethel used to teach...the socialist ideas... Miss Sharland, Janet Tillett and Mr Oxley would...teach separate classes...the history of socialism...for about an hour... It was all very interesting, I enjoyed our little afternoon talks. We could talk about anything we wanted...about 30 or 40 of us.*

In 1911 the Kingsley Hall was opened by Keir Hardie and formed another important meeting place for the Socialists. The building, originally an old manor house, was bought by the Independent Labour Party and, with the aid of voluntary workers and the Bristol branch of the Fabian Society, was transformed from the Conservative Club to a centre for Labour and Socialist activity. (7) Jim Flowers, a life-long socialist, recalls his attendance at the Socialist Sunday school there in 1915 :

> *There was a big hall and a lesser hall upstairs and all our meetings were in the lesser... We used to sing various socialist hymns... 'Jerusalem', 'The Internationale' and 'The Red Flag'... There was always a piano there... About six teachers... You sit in different corners of the room, all different ages in together, and talk about some aspect (of socialism)... Usually in the Young Socialists there was a thin paper magazine which used to come out monthly... It was more or less about brotherhood. I wouldn't say it was the sort of socialism that I understand today, but it was a very humane, brotherly love and you know the pictures used to be of lambs gamboling about all over the place and children playing around, parents looking benignly on them, that sort of thing, very friendly...(8)*

Souvenir

of

"The Great Adventure"

"CASEY" (Walter Hampson)

The Programme is on the following page

Similarly, Edie Hill remembers her experience of Socialist Sunday School in Cobden Street:

> *He (father) sent us to these schools...so that we should learn the rudiments of it (socialism)... There was a meeting place in Cobden Street... Over the Labour Rooms it was only like a little shop and we used to go down there to a socialist class, and a Mr Rossiter used to teach us about socialism... "Each for all and all for each"...about collective buying to make things easier for the very, very poor... He used to encourage us to read Socialist literature...sing songs... He was an ordinary working man.*

The childhood reminiscences of other elderly Socialists suggest that this alternative culture was distinctive, and placed a strong emphasis on the education of Socialist principles. Popular books and newspapers which were present in their homes were those written by Robert Blatchford, Jack London, Robert Tressell, George B. Shaw, poetry, especially the 'Penny Poet' series, 'The Clarion', 'Justice' and 'Reynold's Paper', to name but a few. Apart from books, many small and informative pamphlets existed which could be bought very cheaply, such as the 'Popular Propaganda Socialist Pamphlets' produced by the Socialist Labour Press, Edinburgh, for the price of one penny. The reader could choose from twenty topics such as 'The Class Struggle', 'Socialism From Utopia to Science', and potted versions of essays by Engels and Marx. (9)

Socialist parents recognised the importance of educating their children along Socialist lines, as the state provided education focussed upon the celebration of imperialism, and the inculcation of obedience and deference. (10) In 'The Child's Socialist Reader' the substance of the text aimed to stimulate a critical awareness of society and its inequalities. For example, the list of contents reads, 'What is Socialism; Happy Valley: A Fairy Tale; Karl Marx; Environment: A Story of Two Pictures; The Raid of Gold: Economic Story; William Morris; The Two Steamers: A Story with a Meaning'. The following is an extract from the Two Steamers.

> *In the steamer 'Capitalism' there was a magnificent dining saloon, all decorated with gold and white carving, a music saloon with a piano and an organ, a ladies' saloon with soft couches... But in the third class matters were much worse. Nearly 400 people lived, ate and slept in a space and under conditions to which on shore we would not expose dumb animals to. On the Steamer 'Socialism' everything was differently arranged...(11)*

Socialist books both new and second-hand, newspapers, and pamphlets could be bought at Jack Flynn's shop in the Haymarket in the late nineteenth and early twentieth century. Flynn's shop was a socialist rendezvous and in 1896 the Bristol Socialists produced a series of 'socialist bombs' there. The 'bombs' were short verses printed on small sheets and many thousands were distributed. From that date on, the shop was nick-named the 'Bomb Shop'. Jim Flowers recalls the shop where he took the 'Socialist Standard', which Jack Flynn would sell:

> *His shop...right on the corner...now covered by Marks and Spencers. Opposite Marks and Spencers was a big open space called the Haymarket... There was railings all round...tarmac in the middle... They used to have outdoor meetings there. He used to sell cigarettes and things like that, and he was a cripple... He used to sell the 'New Leader' or the ILP paper and 'The Free Thinker'. He was always sat behind the counter and they used to have discussions in his room right behind, and he used to have a lot of second-hand books.*

Jim Flowers also recalls the christening ceremony which replaced the traditional religious ritual. In fact the christening of his baby brother 'Rev' short for revolutionary at the Kingsley Hall caused a rumpus in the local press:

> *The secretary and the chairman used to sit at the table and the teachers and all the kiddies were in there... And the baby was laid out and perhaps a song would be sung...'The Internationale'... Somebody would be playin' the piano, see, and somebody would say a few words... 'We now accept this new human into our ranks'. The youngest one would lay a posy of flowers...and the next one...and they'd finish up with about twelve little bunches of flowers on it you see.*

For the Bristol Socialists, 'socialism was a movement inspired by art as well as economics'. Records of the society illustrate that recitations, music and poetry - particularly that of John Gregory - made the meetings 'whole'. (12) The Bristol Movement had its own workman composer, J. Percival Jones, who composed and adapted old melodies and tunes to fit socialist songs. Like the more famous national figures, Morris and Carpenter, the Bristol socialists wrote their own songs and Rose Sharland, E.J. Watson and John Gregory each had songs printed. Gregory's 'Who to Make a Merrie England' consistently appears in pamphlets and on handbills and propaganda sheets, which were sometimes distributed at large meetings and demonstrations, and was the song chosen to open the Social Democratic Party's 29th Annual Conference held in Bristol in 1909. (13)

Of course this use of poetry and song to inspire a sense of solidarity and identity and to stimulate emotion stems from a long tradition of hymnology, particularly that of Methodism. Similarly, Chartism had left a rich source of poetry and ballads from which the Socialist poets drew the basic imagery of poverty, inequality and oppression. The following are the first two verses of 'Who to Make a Merrie England', which show the influence of both Christian hymnology and Chartism; but the worship of God is replaced with the worship of Love, emphasising the values and principles of socialism.(14)

> *Who to make a merrie England,*
> *Will be with us in a fight*
> *To dethrone the monster, Mammon?*
> *Who with us, for Love's delight,*
> *Will be comrades, faithful comrades,*
> *In the strife for human right?*
>
> *We will make a happy England;*
> *We will free it from foul dread*
> *Of that poverty which bringeth*
> *Lack of Love, and want of bread;*
> *Shame shall cover us all over,*
> *While our children are unfed.*

The energy and enthusiasm which the Bristol Socialists devoted to creating poetry and song as a means of personal expression and as a means of reinforcing class consciousness led to a widespread recognition and admiration for their talents. Several had works published. (15) Besides artistic activities, many other entertainments and social events were organised. Fund raising bazaars and fetes, concerts, pantomimes, dances and whist sessions were frequent occurences as well as the summer rambles. (16) John Wall's eldest daughter, Ethel, a teacher of piano and mandolin, put on many concerts. All the Wall family took part in these concerts, singing or reciting and, although these events were not exclusively for socialists, many attended them at the Shepherd's Hall, the Wellington Hall Mission and St James's Hall.

One fund raising event which was organised entirely by the Bristol Socialist Society was the 'Libertie Fayre' in 1911. The members construced a 'Mediaeval English Village' - 'something akin to the village William Morris pictured' describes the booklet produced to advertise the Eastertide event. The two-day fair was set in Castle Green Council School, opposite the site of the old Bristol Castle, and was opened by Ben Tillett with Labour Song No. 8. Boots, books, clothes, food and handicrafts all made by the Bristol Socialists were on sale, and a variety of entertainments, including concerts, a play and an orchestra conducted by R. Sharland, took place. (17).

THE SUNDAY RESEARCH AND RECREATION SOCIETY

IN CONJUNCTION WITH

The Workers' Educational Association.

The undermentioned Series of SUNDAY MORNING LECTURES will be delivered

At the SOCIETY ROOMS, BROAD STREET, at 10.45.

Mr. LAURIE MAGNUS, M.A., will deliver a course of Six Lectures on "The Highway of The Renaissance,"

On SUNDAYS, Jan. 18th, Feb. 1st and 15th, March 1st, 15th, and 29th, 1914, at 10.45.

The course will include—

"THE ROADS OUT OF THE MIDDLE AGES." (1) Humanism. (2) Discovery. (3) Dissent. The first Humanist—Petrarch. Camoëns—the Poet of the Portuguese Navigators. The Precursors of the Reformation : Valla. Pico della Mirandola. Reuchlin.

"IDEALS AND REALITIES." The "Romance of the Rose" Traditions. Froissart. Villon. Politian and Savonarola in the Florence of Lorenzo de' Medici. Ariosto and Machiavelli. Luther and Pope Leo X. Castiglione and Rabelais.

"RENAISSANCE MISSIONARIES." Sir Thomas More. Erasmus. Colet. Sir Philip Sidney. Italy and England. Shakespeare's Triumph.

ADMISSION FREE.

VISITORS CORDIALLY INVITED.

QUESTIONS AND DISCUSSION.

GEO. GORDON & SON, TYP., 19, OLD KING ST. BRISTOL.

Clearly the Bristol Socialists, who numbered several hundred, were a minority group in which a nucleus of dedicated activists organised meetings, propaganda and entertainment. Although they supported all the labour disputes, strikes and locked-out workers during the difficult years of the 90s and early twentieth century, they retained their identity as a distinct and influential body. In the huge May Day demonstration of 1890 Socialists brought up the rear. As one socialist remarked 'There goes the procession, winding its way like a serpent through the narrow streets, but the sting is in its tail!' (18)

Many of them conceived Socialism as a religion in which 'brotherliness' and 'love of humanity' were the foundations upon which a more humane and just society could be built. In the 'Souvenir Booklet of Favourite Quotations' compiled by the Society's secretary Sam Bale, national and local activists contributed political and poetic quotations for each day of the year. For example:

> 30 August. Stubbing, J.A. London.
> Our hope-The young.
> Our faith - Ourselves.
> Our religion - Humanity.

> 28 August. Butler, Joe.
> Success to the Bristol Socialist Society Libertie Fayre. May it be the means of hastening the overthrow of the present miserable abortion called Society, and establishing a new world, the foundations of which shall be Justice, and Love the spirit of its inhabitants. (19)

These qualities had to come from within the individual as well as from structural changes within society and John Sharland, a pioneer of the Bristol Socialists, who was elected onto the city council in 1893, refused to attend Mansion House banquets and luncheons, perceiving the inherent contradiction of his participation in such affairs.

Many of the Bristol Socialists were anti-royalist, and John Gregory produced a pamphlet called 'The Jubilee Humbug' which was distributed during the demonstration protesting against expensive civic arrangements for the celebration of Queen Victoria's reign in 1887. This was a time of great stress for the local working people who were experiencing mass umeployment, lock-outs or casual labour and their misery and poverty, described in the *Special Commission - The Homes of the Bristol Poor* just three years previously, were still very much in the minds of the Bristol Socialists. The following is an extract from the 1884 report:

> In...St Jude's we come into contact with scores of further illustrations of
> the squalor and wretchedness of the majority of 'homes' in this district...

Stepping into one...we find a dingy room with a stone floor, and one bed, on which have been found sleeping the man, his wife and four children... The place is used for the manufactory of sweetmeats...hawked about the street by the man and woman. The boy and girl are shoeless and tattered... The adjoining room is occupied by a husband, wife and five children; the husband (is) a baker, only obtaining casual employment, and sometimes only earning sixpence a day. (20)

Similarly, many Socialists were pacifists who believed that Socialism was an international movement - to spread world peace was as important as liberating the workers from the tyranny of the Capitalist system. Imperialism and jingoism were abhorred by many in the Bristol group: Sam Bale (an historian who wrote under the name S. Bryher) kept his daughter home from school Empire Day celebrations. (21) At the 29th Annual Conference of the Social Democratic Party, held in Bristol in 1909, several delegates appealed to parents not to encourage militarism by allowing their children to join Baden-Powell's Scouts and the conference also sent its greetings to many races and people of Hindustan, wishing them early emancipation from the despotic and ruinous domination of Great Britain'. (22)

In Bristol the relationship between the Socialist Society and other organisations with similar aims had always been good, but when a local branch of the ILP was formed in 1893, the older body of Socialists was cautious. The ILP during its formative years had dropped the word 'socialism' from the party's official title in its attempt to disassociate itself from connections with 'revolutionary' socialism, and this had displeased some members of Socialist organisations. In 1900, the Labour Party emerged from the Trades Union Congress of the previous year, and Ramsay MacDonald was asked to draft out a constitution. Again the SDF, with whom the Bristol Socialists were affiliated were anxious. H. Quelch, a delegate of the SDF proposed a resolution acknowledging that 'socialism' would remain the ultimate aim of the Labour Party, but an amendment to this proposal left many of the delegates suspicious and dissatisfied. (23)Although there were some members of the Bristol group who lent towards the Labour Party and reformist politics, most of the Society supported the feelings of the SDF who saw the need for the thorough education of the working class from within. Class war was in some ways opposed to the socialist principles of 'brotherliness' and 'love', and the 'sentimental socialists' hoped that conflict might be avoided in the creation of a socialist society. At the 1901 Conference of the Socialist Democratic Party (which had absorbed the SDF) it was decided to send fraternal greeting to the ILP... Trusting that the deliberations of both will lead to the growth and consolidation of socialist forces...and a speedy consummation of the socialist revolution.' The decision illustrated an underlying tension between the two. (24)

At the conference one delegate proposed that Will Thorne, a Labour MP, should resign from the SDP remarking that 'his dual position was harmful and illogical to the party'. However, another point of view was that the SDP needed its 'outposts'- the majority voted that they should remain. At the conference much discussion ensued on the question of affiliation with the Labour Party but the recommendation was rejected 125 to 2 against. One London delegate proclaimed that the Labour Party was in its present constitution 'anti-social' and should be contested, to which Mr H. Quelch replied that, 'The business of the SDP was...to organise the working classes into a political party... Their object was a fixed one and their principles were definite...not to fight people so much as to win them to Socialism'. (25)

Following the conference in 1909, preparations were made by the Bristol Socialists to run a Socialist candidate in Bristol South - J.F. Green - and at one of the large meetings in the Empire Music Hall he addressed the audience, defining the position of the Bristol Socialists:

> *If they (the audience) believed in political action in order to remedy the wrongs...it was absolutely necessary they should take independent political action... Socialists aimed at the overthrow of the capitalist system and the establishment...of a real co-operative commonwealth...They were perfectly prepared to bring about the change without red-ruin and the break up of laws, but admitted that the change may not be brought about without.*

John Wall, Shoemaker Poet

This next section is an attempt to bring some recognition to a remarkable Bristol shoemaker and socialist poet, John William Henry Wall, 1855-1915. He was born, as he used to say, 'in the shadow of the castle' (site of Bristol Castle), near Mary-le-Port street, in a small row of terraced cottages. (26) He was, during his lifetime, an active supporter of the co-operative movement, instigating one of the first 'co-op' stores; General Secretary of the Boot Cutters Union; Secretary of the Bristol Trades Council; founder of the Bristol Poineers Boot and Shoe Productive Society; and an ardent promoter of education for the working man and woman, organising free evening class scholarships for working people. (27)

Besides these duties and commitments, which frequently took place outside his daily work as a clicker (28), John Wall wrote novels, romances, short stories, songs and poems. Frequently his writings focused upon class inequality, particularly the 'ogres' of unemployment and poverty. He wrote short articles for publication in magazines and newspapers (29) and also had some poems printed in the 'Bristol Observer'. His writing reflects his deep love of history -

both fact and legend - especially relating to the City of Bristol, and of mediaevalism, in which his extensive reading of Scott and the Romantics like Byron, Shelley and Keats powerfully influenced him. (30)

In addition to the writing, Wall conscientiously preserved record accounts, reports, press cuttings and correspondence relating to his social, political and literary activities. For example, he made copies of letters he sent, kept letters he received and even wrote short historical accounts of the two societies he pioneered. (31) In fact, Wall's history of the Bristol and District Co-operative Society was used by Edward Jackson in his book *A Study in Democracy: An Account of the Rise and Progress of Industrial Co-operation in Bristol*. The 'history' was also posthumously published in the co-operative magazine 'Counterpoint'. Some of Wall's life's work (the bulk of which remains unknown) has survived to enrich our knowledge of class struggles in Bristol in the late nineteenth and early twentieth centuries. Its survival is mainly due to the love and devotion of his daughter, Dorothy, whose admiration and belief in the political message of her father's work led her to preserve this valuable collection of writings and documents.

It does not seem premature, in this introduction, to stress the important fact that valuable *unpublished* writings do exist and are in jeopardy of being irrevocably lost. Wall's writing accentuates the precarious future of the memoirs and writings of working people. Because our studies are so frequently geared to the published or printed work, our belief in the paucity of working class culture, with particular reference to creative writing, is perpetuated. And, although Martha Vicinus has shown in her study of nineteenth century literature that it is not uncharacteristic, particularly from members of the artisan class, to have written and published poetry, her study can pay tribute only to those poets who achieved 'success'. These, however, frequently aided by a middle-class benefactor, usually experienced a transient taste of fame and glory. (32)

Furthermore, in the course of my research, I was interviewing an 82 year old daughter of a boiler-stoker, and she informed me that had I called a month earlier I could have seen her father's large collection of books, poetry and writing which, having occupied the front room since her childhood, had recently been removed by the corporation dustman. (33)

We must, therefore, be on our guard against the loss of these potential gold mines, which are embedded in working class culture, and devise ways of searching them out. (34)

I wish also to bring to notice the diverse and unorthodox routes of exploration into collections similar to Wall. Inter-related areas of interest can be uncovered in which the knowledge of those interested in history, literature and art can be mutually enriched; for example, the manner in which Wall, as a working man of very modest means, bringing up a family of six, would use any available scrap of paper upon which he drafted his poems and novels. Letters,

THE
Shakespeare Boot Mart.

" HANG NOTHING BUT A CALF'S SKIN, MOST SWEET LOUT."
King John, Act 3, Scene 1.

JOHN W. H. WALL,

(Late Manager Co-operative Boot Stores, 116, Cheltenham Road)

Begs to inform his friends and the public generally,
that he has opened business in

CROYDON ST., EASTON ROAD,

and can offer

Good Value in Ladies'
Good Value in Gents'
Good Value in Girls' and Boys'

WALKING BOOTS & SHOES,

SLIPPERS, CRICKET & SAND SHOES,

IN ALL THE

Newest Shapes,
Latest Styles,
Best Fittings,

At extremely Moderate Prices for Cash.

Bespoke Orders and Repairs carefully attended to.

EVERY PART OF THE BUSINESS UNDER MY DIRECT OVERSIGHT.

THE FAVOUR OF A CALL IS EARNESTLY SOLICITED.

Note the Address—

THE SHAKESPEARE BOOT MART.
CROYDON STREET, EASTON ROAD.

Chappell, Printer, Redcliff Street.

envelopes, posters, advertisements, propaganda sheets and leaflets of meetings, discussions, debates both political and recreational, formed the bulk of Wall's writing paper. Even thread cards and boot lace packets advertising his trade were used, each card displaying one stanza of a poem. By using each scrap, as an essential piece in constructing the jig-saw puzzle of this man's life, I was able to build up pockets of information relating both to the personal and public life of John Wall and the more general class nature of life in Bristol. In Wall's life, socialism, co-operation and the church to some extent, overlapped and he conceived socialism as a 'practical form of Christianity'. (35) Consequently, Wall's increasing disaffection with the Baptist faith, in which he was brought up, and his embracing of Unitarianism, led him to write some interesting theological expositions.

John Wall left Castle Green Day School at the age of 13 and was apprenticed to become a clicker in the boot and shoe trade. A clicker cut the 'uppers' or leather top part of the boot and shoe, which were composed of six distinct pieces. To cut these out with the minimum waste of leather was a skillful task and the clicker was often considered the 'aristocrat' of the various processes involved. (36) The term 'clicker' was possibly derived either from the noise of the sharf knife used to cut around the zinc patterns or was a derivative of the French word *claquer*, to snap or smack.

The boot and shoe trade in Bristol, although one of the 'newer industries' which experienced a revitalisation in the late nineteenth century, was comparatively late in experiencing mechanisation. Whilst many factories existed in the inner-city areas, they were technologically backward and operated a 'putting out' and sweated labour system in which employers were under no obligation to provide a week's work, or indeed any work at all. (37) In fact Wall's friend, fellow socialist poet and shoemaker John Gregory, well known locally, earned less than three shillings and sevenpence per week. 'Like others at that time he had a 'hard job to make a living' and it is on record at one meeting of the Bristol Trades Council he had made a computation of his wage. Over a period of many weeks...'his earnings had not reached an average of 3/7d. per week and he had to be at his shop waiting for work like a fisher at a stream waiting for a bite'.(38) The boot and shoe industry was one of the most insecure and irregular forms of employment in Bristol during the late-nineteenth and early-twentieth centuries, subject to fluctuations in supply and demand. Kingswood, for example, was an area which specialized in the production of hob-nail boots and when trade was brisk 100 tons were produced weekly. However, the Kingswood trade supplied boots to the South Wales tinplate industry, and when slumps occurred there the bootmakers found themselves temporarily out of work or on three-quarters time.

In the 1892 lockout, resulting from a long-standing pay award which was disputed by the employers, 30,000 workers were affected. The lock-out tactic was enforced to starve the workers into submission. The boot-makers' eventual victory, however, undermined the employers to the extent that one Kingswood manufacturer, Messrs Jay Bros., in a dispute later that year, dismissed all union men and refused to employ unionists. Another manufacturer opposed the pay award and threatened to move his factory out of Bristol. In the winters of 1895 and 1898, three to four thousand operatives connected with the industry in East Bristol were unemployed for several weeks and relief funds were set up to prevent starvation of families without food or fire. (39) It was conditions such as these which led Wall to search for an alternative, more humanitarian way of production and distribution. Clearly his short stories and novels, which are probably semi-autobiographical, reveal his hatred of the tyranny of the factory system. Petty rules and regulations, piece work, excessive hours of work and the despicable situation of competition between fellow men and women to secure and retain employment, were some of the evils he described in 'The Murder of Ada Collins: True Stories of the People'. In this short story, written in a lively way reminiscent of Dickens, Wall interweaves a tragic romance with incisive social comment on the tyrannies of a late-nineteenth century boot and shoe factory.

> *Under the old regime the foremen were 'jolly good fellows every one', who did not kick, if they heard that a hand was going into the office to beg a favour of the 'guv'nor'. On the contrary, if the case was a deserving one they helped it forward: When there was a doubt about it - well! Even then they never cut mean. But now! all this was changed... Saxton's entrance into the cutting room was the signal for talking to cease. There was a time when this was not so. In the days of yore the men had been accustomed to chat a little over their work. It helped the time away without interfering with the work... The late foreman thought so too; for he never interposed unless it were to check irregularity or objectionable language. Sometimes he would join in the discussion. But the new man quickly altered all this... 'Talking interferes with the despatch and finish of the work...And so do singing and whistling'... Thus it was that in Saxton's presence the clicking room became as silent as a mortuary.*
>
> *I must first explain the economy of a clicking room... To those who know, the whole system is comprehended in two intelligent words - 'Grinding' and 'Costing'. 'Grinding' is getting the greatest amount of work done for the lowest amount of wage. 'Costing' is ascertaining how much work has been cut out of a given piece of material or skin. Uppers are cut in pairs. 'How many this week?' and 'Does your costing pay?' are two questions which are periodically, if surreptitiously, asked in the cutting shops of Bristol and the district. The man who can cut the largest number of pairs per week is known as a 'slogger': he who can get the most out of a skin is considered the best or most clever workman. Every employer has a laudable desire to place his goods in the market as*

cheaply as possible commensurate with quality - How is he to do this? Here is one way - By curtailing the wage-sheet. This is the justification - the only justification, for overseers. They are paid to regulate and organise, to keep the workpeople at their tasks and reduce the expenses of the departments over which they have charge. To accomplish these points the foremen of some clicking-room summon to their aid the labours of two men, the 'slogger' and the clever workman. When they have ascertained what the one can cut per week, and the other per skin, they expect the rest to produce the same. If they cannot, they are told either that they have not earned their money, or that their costings do not pay. These are the effectual weapons to weed them out or reduce their wages. But there is another weapon open to the overseer. He may set up an imaginary standard to which even the quickest and the most skilled cannot attain. This is incontrovertibly proved by the dual fact, that although clickers have been at no time more quick and skilled than at the present, yet wages all round are lower, now than they ever were, and still on the decline.

Wall as an idealistic young man believed that these conditions had arisen partly through selfish and tyrannical individuals, such as overseers, whose job was intrinsically exploitative. He was attracted to 'co-operation' as an alternative to the capitalist economic structure which was geared to money-making and exploitation. Wall's concern focusses upon the alienation of individuals from each other, as much as an alienation from their work or craft. He stresses the necessity of friendship and consideration in the work situation in order to generate feelings of equality and justice between employer and workers. The basis of Wall's perhaps rather idealistic belief was firmly rooted in Christian notions of love and brotherhood and Wall was at this time a regular attender at the Old King Street Baptist Church.

Employers! Invite the confidence and trust of those who are giving their prime labour to enrich you. Show yourselves their friends, their guides. Make them your true helpers - your co-workers. It has been done successfully in France, at Paris and at Guise. Why not in Bristol? Then 'snakes'* and 'tale-bearers' and 'frauds'* would gradually die out. There would be no place for them. Foreman and leaders we shall always need and in the ranks of our industrial army are many qualifying for the very front of the vanguard of our future, if their manhood is not crushed out by the evils of the system under which they labour at present. (40)

Thus Wall turned to Co-operation and, whilst Secretary of the Bristol Trades Council in 1883, organised a series of talks for Autumn 1883 and

* Titles of a chapter in the story 'The Murder of Ada Collins' by John Wall

Winter 1884, including one on Co-operation. He arranged for Canon Percival at Trinity College, Oxford, (one time headmaster of Clifton College) to speak at *The Star* coffee house, Old Market, where the council ran its meetings. Percival's inspiring lecture, 'Some Ways in Which Trade Unions May Help' and, later, G.F. Jones's lecture on 'Co-operation', boosted the determination and idealism of Wall and his colleagues. The outcome of these talks was that Wall and four others formed the Bristol and District Co-operative Society (the 'B and D'), establishing a small co-op store. In a letter to Canon Percival, dated 15 February 1884, Wall informed him of their resolution:

> *You will be pleased to learn that we are making an attempt to place the co-operative principle on a practical footing in Bristol... A veteran Co-operator, Mr Williamson, (who was secretary for many years of the late Bristol Industrial and Provident Co-operative Society), Mr Hams and myself talked the matter over and came to the conclusion that the time had arrived when an attempt should be made to re-establish Co-operation in the old City... Any advice from you would be especially welcomed by all of us, because we know the practical interest you take in the subject and because you are an old friend of the Bristol working man.*

At Wall's home in Croydon Street on Tuesday, 26 February, a small company assembled consisting of Wall and his father-in-law James White, H.A. Carter and G.W. Ham and, in Wall's own words they passed 'a resolution pledging (us) to plank down one shilling each for a bundle of literature from the Co-op Union...to arrange for an early meeting at "The Star"...(and) to ask the Central Board to send down a couple of Speakers...to give us advice and awaken interest in the movement'. (41)

The Co-operators were loaned an office by Gilmore Barnett for subsequent meetings having gained new recruits at the opening of the Co-operative Wholesale Society Depot. The group were then able to be in 'business', with 48 members and £40. (42) The Society began its career at Houlton Street in November 1884 and Wall recorded the opening evening of the store:

> *We can never forget it! The quaint shop, the small counters, the meagre supply of groceries and provisions - in all nineteen articles which had cost us £20. 'Money down on your first order', said Mr Cunningham, who waited on us at the depot... The Committee, inexperienced yet willing, with white aprons tied on firmly, bustling around with...the importance, but also the love of a mother hen with her first brood.*

The store opened for six months, two nights a week, and members of the Committee voluntarily served behind the counter. During the first quarter the average weekly trading amounted to £10 and, at the end of the first quarter, takings amount to £130 with a 'divi' of 1/6d. The balance was carried forward enabling the store to open during the day time. After nine months and a drastic reduction in the dividend and loss in trade the storekeeper was changed. John Wall, then secretary, incorporated this office with that of storekeeper and moved into the premises at Houlton Street. An improvement occurred and after a very successful meeting in Canon's Marsh Workmen's Coffee Room new members were recruited. A branch store was subsequently opened in St Georges Road, Hotwells and Lawrence Hill. In February 1887, the Houlton Street store moved to new premises in Newfoundland Road and became the Registered Office and Central Store.

Wall was involved with the 'B and D' for four years, working as a paid member for three. During this time he gave up the secretaryship, working on as storekeeper and accountant, but the rigorous demands of a 75-hour week led him to resign his post in the summer of '87.

> *I beg to give a fortnight's notice from Saturday next to my intention to leave your employ. My reason for taking this decisive step is simply on account of the excessive number of hours I have to devote to a conscientious performance of my official duties... When I gave up the secretaryship, I was hoping with you the effect would be such a diminution of work which would enable me to accomplish the remainder in work hours. In this hope I find myself disappointed, the two journeys per week to the Stores and the Bank and now the time occupied in attending to the bakehouse have enormously increased the time I have to devote to my duties. Last week I partly remedied this by excluding myself as much as possible from Store work - the effect being that Mr Hodge and the young man were at high pressure the whole of the time, and much work such as cleaning and tidying the Store...had to be neglected. But notwithstanding this I had to be at the work no less than 75 hours at the lowest computation. And...this a Holiday Week!*

Although Wall resigned from the 'B and D' he continued as a committee member, for his enthusiasm for the co-operative ideal remained strong. He returned to his house in Croydon Street and set up his own little boot shop in the front room, calling it the Shakespeare Boot Mart. He had a small hut at the back of the house containing his equipment for making boots and shoes, and also did repairs; he remained here until his death in 1915. Frequently people would drop in for a chat and Wall's youngest daughter Dorothy remembers the Rev. Paul Stacey, who spent many hours talking to John Wall in his shop where he said he felt 'most inspired'.

In October 1888, however, another co-operative venture was born - the Bristol Pioneers' Boot and Shoe Productive Society.

> *In the fall of the year Mr F. Gilmore Barnett gathered a small company of working men together to discuss the possibility of introducing Productive Co-operation into Bristol… (Eventually) the following scheme was adopted as expedient. Mr Barnett agreed to lend the sum of £100 for seven years to four men upon the express conditions.*
> *1. That interest should be paid half yearly.*
> *2. That 50% of the net profit should be divided amongst the workers in proportion to their earnings. It will be readily seen that these conditions combined business with sentiment.* (43)

In November John Wall became Secretary of the Pioneers and they set up a small workshop in Twinnell Street, Easton, buying machinery and materials. Initially trade was bad, but in the following August the Society was registered under the Industrial and Provident Act of 1876 becoming a limited liability society. Trade gradually improved and in 1892 the Society moved to Kings Square. Within four years the membership increased from nine to seventy. The Society operated at a loss, but Wall was convinced that with careful management and increased trade they would be able to achieve their goal of bringing dividend to custom and labour.

Wall's interest in co-operation was not just for the material gains in the form of the 'divi'. It was based on an idealistic yearning for a sound and just form of economic production and distribution. The aim of Wall's co-operative venture was to supply good quality articles cheaply in reasonable and fair working conditions. These conditions were dictated by the workers themselves who had contributed a nominal sum to initially finance the venture.

Eventually Wall came to the conclusion that Co-operation was in fact a 'red herring', unlike Trade Unionism which was engaged in direct class struggle over the wages and conditions of workers.

In 1887 he wrote to the editor of Co-op News, arguing that deeper issues were involved concerning changes in attitude if Co-operation was to succeed as an egalitarian movement:

> *It is not enough for Co-operators to say to the workman, 'We employ you and pay you a fair market rate of wage. You are therefore our servants and on the whole your hours of work are shorter than those of the workers outside the movement. What more do you want?'… What it seems to me is a bold recognition of the sacredness of labour.* (44)

Wall explains in his letter that the 'sanctity of labour' involves not only a more equal distribution of wealth, but also of *leisure,* so that the worker can explore the Fine Arts, write or study botany or any other interest he may wish pursue. Wall's hatred of inequality is expressed in his poem 'the Individualist'. His indictment of the capitalist system and competitive individualism illustrates the poverty and the inequality of the workers in industrial society.

THE INDIVIDUALIST

Look not into our face again, false man!
Who hast betrayed thy trust for love of gold.
Count up the tale of those thy Plan has slain -
Of needy women, men and children too;
And all to win a house upon a hill:
To write a name upon a civic roll;
Or to be mentioned in a birthday list 'Who's Who'.

Say Watts! Say Stevenson! Say all of you,
Whose brows have paled before your study lamps;
If 'twas for these ye bent your heads and worked:-
To build a wall where none before was built?
To make the poor more poor, the rich more rich?
To stamp Despair for ever on the hearts
Of homely common folk? And Murder Love? Tell me?

Tell me if 'twas for these ye gave the Loom
To us, the telegraph, the power in steam,
The apparatus to explore a mine
When Fire and Afterdamp have ruin spread,
The Locomotive, the Electric Car?
Was it for these ye sought to bind the winds
Fast to balloons, and to the gear of aeroplanes?

O Ghosts of these I name and other Ghosts,
Whose working thought on earth was Brotherhood,
Breathe not too hard against the selfish man
When he shall join you in the Sphere Beyond.
Yet if some punishment must be his due
Let him be 'cabined' in the gloom, and let
Him feel something of that he made the workers feel.

We eat of poverty - because his plan
Can pluck the fruit of life away from us:
We dwell in misery - because his plan
Reserves Life's Fullness for an Idling Class.
Then let him feel awhile, I say, the pain
We've known so long. Not for revenge, O no!
But that his Ghost at least may turn to Brotherhood.

Clearly Wall's rejection of capitalism was not rooted in any naive yearning for a return to a pre-industrial society, for he fully recognises the advantages and potential of modern technology. The problem was that these technological advances were expropriated by a ruling class and by selfish individuals who exploited the workers. When Wall wrote this poem Bristol was notorious for sweated labour, and in the 'rag trade' for example women's costumes costing 1/1d. to produce were being sold for 39/-. (45) The poem clearly illustrates Wall's 'Christian Socialism' for in the last stanza he does not suggest a torturous end for the entrepreneur who exploited his employees but that he should be spiritually awakened so that his soul at least may turn to 'brotherhood'.

A further criticism of capitalism - one which Wall had personally experienced - was the competition for labour between young and old. Experience of unemployment and rejection led him to write an essay, 'Too Old at Forty', reflecting on the psychological as well as the material evils of this type of competition.

> *We become unpopular with the people who employ labour. When we answer an advertisement they look dubiously at the 'tokens of honour' appearing on our heads, the 'lines of experience' crossing our faces, the 'mellowed way' we walk into the office. And straightway they shake their heads in the peculiarly decisive way we are getting used to, 'How old did you say? My dear fellow you won't do! What we require is a young man - strong, alert... Send your son along and we'll see'... Of course the young must have their work to do as well...it necessary for their efficient training as workmen, as citizens, as teachers, that there should be opportunities ever opening up before them... It appears to me that men are 'too old at 40' or a little older, partly because of the feverish desire of some captains of industry to make a pile quickly; (and) partly because of the anxiety of some directors to secure big dividends for their shareholders. By these people human activities are made subservient to 'piles' and 'dividends'. (46)*

Although there is a note of bitterness in Wall's tone, his characteristic humour always surfaces, revealing the critical but often sensitive and subjective element in his writing style. His use of the metaphor 'tokens of honour' which implies greying hair or perhaps even a bald patch are visual reminders which add to the insecurity and anxiety of the unemployed middle-aged man. The essay also reveals Wall's concern for the social problem of elderly people who become unwanted because they are useless to industry:

> *When they begin to fail by reason of the wear and tear of life, they must be removed from the mechanism of the industrial machinery, thrown aside, and replaced...by others.*

Wall's criticism of capitalism and disillusionment with co-operation, which had become equally ignoble and unjust, was due to the employers and directors who he felt were selfish and exploitative:

> *Although they are so quick to detect the failing strength of others, they never, or rarely ever, acknowledge the inroads of nature upon their own frames. They cling to office as a limpet to a rock…In our papers the other day the resignation was announced of one of these gentry - a director of a public company - at the ripe old age of 98!!*

Wall rejected the 'Self-Help' ethic which popularised the notion that any person could raise themselves up through hard work and avoid hardship and despair. It was a well-worn argument used by the wealthy ruling class to avoid responsibility for the distress and poverty caused by unemployment, low wages and trade recessions. Wall was also aware of the way in which children were duped into an uncritical celebration of bourgeois industrialists in elementary schools, and perceived this inculcation of false consciousness to be partly responsible for the perpetuation of the evils of our society:

> *If we were to ask ourselves seriously how millionaires are made, and who suffer in the making: if the compilers of our school-books were at pains to give some of the 'cons' as well as the 'pros' in the examples of 'Self-made Men' - often meaning 'Wealthy Men'; our outlook would be considerably clarified.*

In this essay Wall suggests that a more equal distribution of physical labour would help to solve the problem of unemployment and all its affiliated evils, so that 'those who now do little or nothing, may lighten the burdens of others by bearing a hand in necessary toil… Of course there would have to be a limitation of the hours of work per day'. In this view he supported the Fabians and gradually drifted from Co-operation towards Socialism and in 1908 he joined the Bristol Socialist Society. (47)

For Wall, socialism was a practical form of Christianity, and he believed that if men and women shared equally work and leisure then a true 'brotherhood' would exist. Wall's socialism was shaped by many varied literary sources. The Chartist movement, in which his Bristolian father-in-law James White participated, influenced him in his youth, together with City Road Young Men's Mission and Working Association. The first provided Wall with literature and the second the experience of poverty. Whilst engaged in 'missionary work' in St Philips and St Judes, Wall gained first hand knowledge of the real poverty and degradation in which many working people lived, and in 1875 he noted in his report: 'God grant that more hearts may be stirred up, who shall not be ashamed to go down in St Philips to labour for

NATIONAL UNION

OF

~~TOP~~ BOOT CUTTERS

Bristol Branch, No. *1*

Dec 7st 1887

SIR,

You are summoned to attend *a*

Committee Meeting of the Branch

at *Elsworð Secretary's House*

on *thursday Dec 10st 1887* at

8 o'clock, for the purpose of *Considering*

important Buisness.

Should you fail to attend or reply to this
note, you will be _____ according
to General Laws.

I am Sir, yours obediently,

A. E. Bragg SECRETARY.

Secretary's Address :

Pembroke House Albany Rd sessess place
st Pauls

Where all communications or complaints must be sent.

Him'. (48) Although the City Road Mission was at heart a 'soul-saving' mission it did provide practical help. The 'brethren' visited homes, offered consolation and gave to the poor and elderly, as well as the usual provision of open air services and bible readings. The area, as reported in the investigation into working-class housing conditions in Bristol in 1884, was rarely visited by people over the 'brethren' or missionaries:

> *Beyond its inhabitants only the clergy and ministers; voluntary visitors to the homes of the poor, and the scripture reader and city missionary...can feel the inexpressible weariness and mental depression...amidst the poor people dwelling in the Marsh and adjoining parts of St Philips.* (49)

This was hardly surprising when the main industries of this area were manure manufactories, bone crushing mills, knackers' yards, horse-flesh boiling factories and chemical works!

These experiences in St Philips provided Wall with a real perspective of poverty and hardship, and his writings, poetry and novels constantly reiterate his desire for equality and brotherhood. Wall was familiar with the literary works of Shakespeare and the Romantics - Scott, Byron, Shelley; historians like Gibbons; and contemporary writers like Eugene Sue and William Morris. Although he was extremely fond of mediaevalism and ancient history, he was not seduced by the literature of Romantics like Keats. For example, he wrote an interesting and humorous exposition on the romantic concept of chivalry and knights in which he quotes from Scott, Masson and Froissart. One key element in much of his writing is the condemnation of war and violence, which is in opposition to his socialist commitment to 'brotherhood'. Thus in his poetry he attacks the romantic image of mediaeval knights riding to battle, and also those writers who celebrate war.

THIS IS THE LAW

> *The sounds of soldiers' footsteps marching through a glen,*
> *The champing bits of many streets, the laugh of men;*
> *And sunbeams brightly shining on the helms and spears,*
> *But - in the villages behind them - Women's tears:*
>
> *For War is not, it never can be, the great thing*
> *Some novelists aver, some little poets sing.*
> *It ever did, and will (this is the Law - you'll find),*
> *Leave a broad trail of blood and ruined homes behind.*
>
> *Each feud will scatter wide the seeds of later feuds,*
> *To yield a reddened harvest for the hungry moods*
> *Of human snarling tigers. Each onset affords*
> *Fresh cause for hate, and ruthlessness, and jangled words.*

John Wall's dream of a peaceful and harmonious society led him to write one of his greatest achievements - a historical romance, set in Thebes, which is similar to Morris's *News from Nowhere* although it is significantly a description of a *peaceful* transformation to a perfect society. However, in spite of this novel, which optimistically informs the reader of the transformation to an egalitarian society, Wall was occasionally plagued by doubt and pessimism about the future. The following poem, with its rather bitter and vehement tone, expresses this despair and suggests that one may in fact only *dream* of a socialist society:

LET ME DREAM

Let me dream of a State - happy, joyous, and full,
For the dreaming is mainly my share,
Since the Worker is thrust from that State, as a rule,
To the other of carking and care:
I know no one can, or ought, to expect
Just Life's good things, and fly from the bad,
Yet idlers of title try hard to collect
To their side every joy to be had.

Let me down - not alone for myself, there are those
Cribbed with me in the gloom. For these too
Let me dream of the Glens, and the sweet mountain rose,
And cirrus-clouds high in the blue:
In my dream there are common lands still undefiled
By the boards - PRIVATE GROUNDS. Let me dream
We can roam where the bluebells and daisies are piled
Or laugh near the loud bubbling stream.

Wall remained with the Pioneers until 1892, in spite of ill-health, and at this time he was earning 33/- per week plus the few extra shillings he picked up from boot repair work in his home-based shop. In 1893, a period of great hardship and unemployment in Bristol, he applied for a job in Nuneaton in a Co-operative Society, but was unsuccessful. The following year he applied for the post of general manager in the commercial department of a newspaper, a job which he possibly felt brought him closest to the atmosphere of his burning ambition - writing and journalism. Again it appears he was unsuccessful and the disappointment he must have felt is conveyed in some of his writing. The obstacles which Wall felt prevented him from achieving his ambition lay in the economic and class structure of society. Most of the working class were deprived of further education and their elementary education was rooted in a conservative ideology which emphasised deference and resignation to one's lot. This form of social control, disguised under the auspices of 'education' was

John Wall's workshop in Kings Square.

a tactic to ensure that the newly enfranchised working-class younger generation would dutifully vote for those who employed and thus controlled them. As local industrialist Sholto Hare put it, they would be 'educated faithfully to perform the franchise'.

Wall's intense fervour for education, which was shared by many radical and socialist groups in the city, arose from the belief that class consciousness and education were necessary for the creation of a Socialist Society. In 1883, whilst secretary for the Bristol Trades Council, Wall organised evening class scholarships for working men and women. These scholarships, largely financed by the Trades' Council, were to be taken at the University College. The issue produced considerable waves of controversy in the local press and one misinformed objector reveals the elitist and fearful attitude of the middle class towards higher education for the workers:

> *Sir, I see from advertisements the University College of Bristol have offered...to the wage earning classes 80 or more scholarships to be held at the University College itself...and of sufficient value to cover fees and buy books... It is an offer to provide gratuitous education...not such education as would be had if the State...were to defray its cost...but absolutely gratuitous...like that of a charity school. The recipients will contribute nothing, nay they will be paid for accepting the boon... Can anything be imagined more demoralising?... It is usually believed that one who feels he is paying his way preserves his self-respect... It is the aim of most judicious philanthropists to avoid giving anything gratis...be it food for the body or the mind - it shall be of the best quality, and sold...it shall always be sold...to depart from this is a serious step in a downward direction.*
> *Anti-Pauperization.* (50).

This letter in response to Wall's attempt to secure a tiny wedge of the educational cake for the workers was seen by Canon Percival, at Trinity College, Oxford. He wrote to Wall offering support and supplied him with some facts with which he could respond to the 'nonsensical letter'. Wall's reply appeared in the Bristol Times and Mirror two days later, informing Anti-Pauperization of his errors in comprehension and logic,

> *Our friend talks about the scheme as being a species of 'charity', and tending to 'pauperise' those who may avail themselves of its provisions...he talks about 'self-reliance' and 'independence' as though these noble attributes will be entirely forfeited by those who benefit from the 'Evening Class Scholarship'. According to his theory, if 'Anti-Pauperization' was educated at either of the great schools, he has long since forfeited his right to be considered as a 'self-reliant and*

independent' man, because he well knows he received his education at about one half of its cost...No member of the middle or upper classes enters Oxford or Cambridge without receiving lodging and education at a rate far below the actual cost. (51)

In spite of Wall's efforts in these directions he remained disillusioned at the lack of educational and social change in the city. Nearly two decades later he wrote of the obstacles which confine and enslave the working man, crushing his potential for creative and imaginative work, or simply curtailing his leisure time and sapping his energy by long working hours. He conceived the frustration of his personal ambitions in terms of oppressive structures of social and economic inequality. In several of his poems Wall refers to himself and other working men as being 'cabined in the gloom'. (52) This phrase taken both literally and metaphorically expresses not only the physical misery and hardship experienced by the workers, but the lack of spiritual or intellectual stimulus which might be experienced if only the working man or woman had more leisure. This pressure Wall felt constantly and attempted to explain to Prof. F.H. Leonard in a letter declining an invitation to discuss his work on a Workers' Educational Association ramble. 'I earn my daily bread making boots and Saturday is the most inconvenient day of the week to get away from the shop.' In a more bitter reflection entitled '49 Today', written in 1904, Wall documents his frustration and resentment:

The middle aged person is restless and pessimistic...and fiercely indignant with the many artificial limitations surrounding him. Ah! who can feel them so keenly as he? Has he not, in the pursuit of his Ideal been fighting them all his lifetime? and still they uprear their walls - grimmer and more giant like than of yore. Upon their battlements are these names - Education, Wealth, Leisure! And woe betide the luckless son of a genius who does not possess at least one of the three - a trained education, a million of money, or much leisure.

The severe conflict between workers, employers and the police during the last decade of the nineteenth century in Bristol, was reflected in an increasing disillusionment and bitterness in Wall's writing. By this time he no longer believed a peaceful transformation to a Socialist Society was possible. The increasing use of violence by the police and military which shocked the citizens of Bristol in 1892-3 finds expression in Wall's poetry of that period, in which the conflict, although still seen in allegorical terms of good versus evil, is in fact class war.

THE LABOUR - GREED CONFLICT

They are spoiling for the fight -
Greed-monger and Labourite

It will be the toughest job you ever saw;
Alexander's Eastern rush,
Wall Street - in a frenzied crush,
Won't be mentioned when these angry foemen drum.

On one's side, see! all the cash,
Greed's defence as well as lash,
Weapons furbished by a century of gains;
Culture - laid on thin like paint,
Education's well known taint -
University acquired, and - all the brains!

On the other side we scan
A defiant working man,
Scorned for long, oft sneered at for a fool,
Who always been content
To trust party government
With his matters since he left the Sunday School.

Now he finds, to his dismay,
He's betrayed, reviled, at bay;
So he slowly turns his sleeves up for the fight.
What're your weapons, simple one?
Justice? Right? Hush! 'Tis begun!
The death dual between Greed and Labourite.

---

(1)   The Socialist movement in Bristol organised in the early 1880s when a branch of Hyndman's Social Democratic Federation was established by a small number of idealistic working men. Withdrawing from the SDF in 1885 after Hyndman had accepted Tory funds to promote political candidates, they formed the Bristol Socialist Society (see S. Bryher). The Labour and Socialist Movement in Bristol, (Bristol 1919) Part 1 pp 7-25.

(2)   Stanley Pierson, Edward Carpenter, Victorian Studies, (March 1970) p312.

(3)   S. Bryher op.cit. pp31,32.

(4)   Ibid p.30,31.
      See also Bristol Sunday Society Poster. John Wall Collection.
      Interview S. Mullen/Mrs Pearce, born 1897, father railwayman.

(5)   Interview S. Mullen/D. Young, teacher bootmaker.
      /Mrs. Pearce, op.cit.
      See also Bristol Socialist Society Labour Songs, inside cover. John Wall Coll.

(6)   Interview S. Mullen/Edie Hill. Factory operative, born 1898, father boilerstoker.

(7)   See Souvenir Booklet of Kingsley Hall, (Bristol 1911) p. 3. J. Wall Collection.

(8)   Interview S. Mullen/Jim Flowers. Lathe turner, born 1905, father lathe turner.

(9)   See pamphlet 'Historical Materialism', Socialist Labour Party. (Edinburgh 1902) J. Wall Collection.

(10) See S. Humphries, 'Hurrah for England' in Southern History: A Review of Southern England. Vol 1, 1979 pp 176-185.

(11) The Child's Socialist Reader. 20th Century Press, Clerkenwell p. 49

(12) S. Bryher part 1, p.24

(13) See the Social Democratic Party booklet on the 29th Annual Conference, (Bristol 1909) p.8. J. Wall Collection.

(14) See Martha Vicinus, The Industrial Muse (1974) for discussion on 19th century working class literature.

(15)   See John Gregory, Idylls of Labour, Murmurs and Melodies (Bristol 1884) My Garden and other Poems (Bristol 1907); Rose Sharland, Voices of Dawn (Bristol 1911); John Wall various poems printed in the Bristol Observer.

(16)   See Bryher. Part 2, pp54,68,74,76.
         Also 29th Annual Conference of SDP booket; Libertie Fayre Booklet, both in Wall collection. See also Bristol Observer April 15th 1911.

(17)   See Libertie Fayre Booklet (Bristol 1911).

(18)   S. Bryher Part 2, p.24.

(19)   Ibid p.73. See also 1911 Libertie Fayre booklet 'Favorite Quotations' p.52.

(20)   The Homes of the Bristol Poor: Special Commissioner of the Bristol Mercury, (1884) p.29.

(21)   Interview S. Mullen/G. Bale, clerk, born 1902, father clerk.

(22)   Bristol Times and Mirror, 12/4/09, p.7

(23)   S. Bryher part 3, pp.5,6,7.
         See also F. Bealey, The Social and Political Thought of the British Labour Party, (Weiderfeld & Nicholson 1970) pp. 1-10.

(24)   Bristol Times and Mirror, 10/4/09. p.3.

(25)   Bristol Times and Mirror, 12/4/09. p.7.

(26)   Interview with Dorothy Young, daughter of John Wall. Born, 1985, Easton Bristol. Schoolteacher. Father, shoemaker.

(27)   See J. Wall collection, deposited in the Bristol Record Office; also, S. Bryher, The Labour and Socialist Movement in Bristol (Bristol 1919) p.13.

(28)   See letter from Paulton 'Clickers' which illustrates the various duties Wall performed whilst secretary for the Boot Top Cutters Union - a letter thanking him for wreaths sent from Bristol for a funeral in Paulton. (Wall collection). See also, The Co-op Society Magazine (June 1957) p.1.

(29)   See manuscripts sent to 'Co-op News' especially 'The Memory of May' (1910) and 'September and some problems' (Oct. 1912) - (Wall collection)

(30)   Wall often emulated the style of Byron and was extremely fond of writing long epics with characteristic Byronesque humour and cynicism.

(31)   The two accounts, one of The Bristol Pioneer Boot And Shoe Productive Society Ltd, and The Bristol And District Co-op Society, together with a short sketch, 'The Manufacture of Boots', all appear in one book contained in the Wall collection. The Co-op Society essay was printed posthumously in Counter Point (1961) pp.7-13.

(32)   See, M. Vicinus, The Industrial Muse (1974) - introduction.

(33)   Interview with Edie Mullen. Born, St. George, 1898.
         Operative in sweet factory. Father, boiler stoker.

(34)   In the 'Bristol People's Oral History Project', many of the old people interviewed wrote down their memories.

(35)   Dorothy Young, 'My Father' p.11 (Wall collection)

(36)   See letter of Paulton 'Clickers', May 13 1884,
         'The funeral did not take place until Monday when the foreman closed the factory, which enabled a lot to follow. The Clickers walked in front then the (or some of the Rounders and Finishers) altogether about 100.' (Wall Collection) See also, A. Fox, The History Of The National Union Of Boot And Shoe Operatives 1874-1957 (1959) p.20

(37)   See R. Whitfield, The Labour Movement in Bristol 1910-1939 (unpublished PhD thesis, University of Bristol, submitted 1979) Part 1, p.36.

(38)   Quoted in Archie Powell, 'Poet and Shoemaker', in Bristol Observer 21 May 1949 p. 2.

(39)   For details of 'sweating' and unemployment in Bristol see - Christian Brotherhood Pamphlet no. 3 Some Facts of Bristol Life (1908) pp.2-4. See also, J. Wall, The Murder of Ada Collins, a short story. (Wall Collection)

(40)   See, Bristol Trades Council Special Meetings Card 1883-1884.

(41)   Co-operative News 1 Feb. 1947 p.6 F. Gilmore Barnett's sympathies were in labour directions, and he did much good service in the cause of the labour movement, especially on the Town Council.

(42)   J. Wall History of The Bristol and District Co-operative Society (1893) pp.7,8. (Wall Collection)

(43)   J. Wall, The History of the Bristol Pioneers Boot and Shoe Productive Society Ltd pp 2,3. (1893) (Wall Collection)

(44)   Letter to the Editor of the Co-op News, titled 'Labour, Capital and Consumption' 16 May 1887 (Wall Collection).

(45)   Some Facts of Bristol Life op. cit. p.3.

(46) J. Wall, 'Too Old At Forty' (1902) pp.3,4,7. (Wall collection)

(47) Letter confirming Wall's membership of the 'Bristol Socialist Society from the secretary S. Bryher.

(48) Secretary's Report for the City Road 'Young Men's Mission', 31 March 1875. (Wall Collection)

(49) Special Commissioner of the Bristol Mercury, *The Homes of The Bristol Poor* (1884) p.51.

(50) *Bristol Times and Mirror* 1 Oct. 1883 p.2.

(51) Letter to Wall from Canon Percival, 2 Oct. 1883 (Wall collection); and *Bristol Times and Mirror* 4 Oct. 1883.

(52) See for example, 'The Individualist' stanza 3 P. 11 (Wall collection)

Trade Unionism in Bristol 1910 - 1926

- Bob Whitfield

Bristol was almost alone among industrial cities in that the four groups of workers who occupy such an important place in the trades union history of the period - dockers, road transport workers, railwaymen and coalminers - were all well represented in the local labour force. Events such as the formation of the Triple Alliance, Black Friday and the General Strike of 1926 all had a special local significance. Much of this article is therefore concerned with the activities of these groups and in particular with the Bristol dockers.

The scope of this article is limited to the period 1910 - 1926. The choice of dates is, of course, an arbitrary one, but there are a number of reasons why this period, a crucial one in the history of trades unions nationally, is worthy of study. The period begins with the revival of trade union membership in the pre-war years and a number of major confrontations between labour and capital in the railways, the docks and in the mining industry. World War One was the occasion for a reduction in the level of industrial conflict, yet, at the same time, trade union membership continued to grow rapidly and the unions succeeded in gaining a greater degree of recognition from employers and the state than ever before. In the post-war years conflict resumed, with the state becoming involved in industrial relations on an unprecedented scale, and the period culminates in the General Strike of 1926 when the state took on the forces of organised labour and defeated them.

It is not the purpose of this article to provide a narrative of the history of trade unions in Bristol during this period. It is an attempt to study a number of important themes in the history of trades unionism from a local perspective.

In 1911 the working population of Bristol numbered some 104,456 males and 59,156 females. (1) The railways provided employment for 3,856 male workers whilst 3,049 were employed in and around the docks and another 2,420 on sea, river and canal transport; 6,028 male workers were engaged in road transport and 2,132 in mining and quarrying. Thus about 17% of the local male labour force were employed in the three key industries in 1911. (This had fallen to about 15½% in 1921 and to about 12½% by 1931.) Numerically therefore, the three key groups did not predominate within the local labour force and were far outweighed by the 8,993 men who were employed in the building industry, the 6,869 men in textile and clothing manufacture, the 3,648 men in boot and shoe manufacturing, the 4,472 in the woodworking and furniture trades and the 3,658 in the printing and paper industries. When the number of women employed in textiles and clothing (11,061), boot and shoes (1,089), printing and paper (4,438) and in the food drink and tobacco industry (8,206) is also taken into account, the relative insignificance of the miners, dockers and the railwaymen in the local labour force appears even more striking. It must also be remembered, that Bristol was an important, and

NATIONAL UNION OF

Boot & Shoe Operatives

The Bristol No 2 Branch.

This Copy of the Monthly Reports is issued by the Council for the use of the Officers and Executive of the above Branch of the Union; the Branch Secretary for the time being to retain possession and upon his retirement it must be handed over by the Branch Committee to the future Secretary,

BY ORDER OF THE COUNCIL.

Leicester, January 1893.

growing, commercial centre and that the 4,625 male clerks in 1911 had increased to 12,686 in 1921 and to 23,602 in 1931, whilst female clerks numbered 5,725 in 1921 and 9,706 in 1931. (2) Also significant among the local labour force were the 12,238 women employed in domestic indoor service in 1911.

From these figures a number of conclusions may be drawn. Firstly, although Bristol may be described as an industrial city, there were large numbers of people who were not engaged in industrial occupations at all and it must be noted that many of those who were employed in manufacturing industry were not working in large factories. In many areas Bristol was honeycombed with small workshops in the clothing, boot and shoe, and furniture industries. Secondly, the most striking point about Bristol's industrial structure was its diversity. No single industry or occupation predominated. This is of obvious importance in considering the trade union history of the city in this period, for although the railwaymen, dockers and miners were key groups of workers within the trade union movement, their influence was out of all proportion to their position within the local labour force. The reasons for this state of affairs provide one of the underlying themes of this article.

From a trade union organiser's point of view, Bristol's industrial structure presented many problems but also offered great opportunities. Skilled craftsmen in the building industry and in the metal trades had a long history of trade union organisation stretching back into the mid-nineteenth century. Bookbinders had had their local trade society as early as 1831. In 1910, however, at the beginning of our period, trade unionists were very much in a minority among the labouring population of Bristol. The general picture was of a number of relatively well-organised trades, surrounded by a mass of workers among whom trades union organisation was weak or non-existent. From the middle of the nineteenth century trade union organisation had been established and consolidated amongst the craftsman in building, engineering and printing and paper industries and, since that time, unionisation had been extended to the railwaymen, miners, clothing, furniture, boot and shoe workers, some dockers, gasworkers, and Corporation workers, but in very few of these industries was trade union membership strong in 1910. Indeed, national organisers in the National Amalgamated Furniture Trades Association (NAFTA) (3) and the National Union of Boot and Shoe Operatives (NUBSO) (4) made frequent complaints at this time that Bristol was a 'blackspot' within the national trades union organisation of their industries.

Craft unions and industrial unions, those which had a clearly indentifiable target group for membership, had been relatively more successful in recruiting members in Bristol before 1910 than had the 'open' unions, which aimed to recruit from among the vast mass of unskilled workers in a variety of trades. Union membership was particularly weak among the unskilled, among women workers, and among those whose employment was seasonal or casual, such as dockers. Union membership was also weak among the workers in the large factories in the confectionery, tobacco, textile, food processing and chemical industries, and was not strong among unskilled workers in the paper bag and packaging factories. During the years of 1889-1892, however, many of the groups of workers listed above were drawn into union membership in an explosion of union activity which followed the victories of the London dockers and gas workers in 1889. The following report, headed 'The Bristol revolt', which appeared in the 'British Workman' in March 1890, gives a glimpse of the events in Bristol and an indication of the multiplicity of trades in which workers in the city were employed.

> *The first strike occurred at Lysaght's galvanised iron works, and this was followed in quick succession by Tinn's galvanised iron workers, the gas workers, the dockers, stay makers, cotton operatives, brush makers, hatters, oil and colour workers, pipe makers, coal carriers, scavengers, box makers, cigar makers, tramway men, hauliers, blue factory workers, animal charcoal workers, etc, etc.* (5)

Many of these early struggles were successful in winning wage increases and union recognition and the years 1889-1892 witnessed the rapid growth of Ben Tillett's Dock, Wharf, Riverside and General Workers Union (DWR & GWU) and Will Thorn's Gasworkers and General Labourer's Union (G & GLU) in Bristol. This movement was noteworthy for a number of reasons. Apart from a brief period in the early 1870s, it was the first occasion since the 1830s on which large numbers of unskilled workers, many of them in casual employment, had been attracted into trade union membership. Women workers, particularly those at the Great Western Cotton Factory, Barton Hill and in the confectionary trade, played a prominent part. The strikers set out, through marches and propaganda, to win public sympathy and much of the work of publicising the strikers' cause was undertaken by the small, but growing, local socialist movement. Prominent among the workers involved in struggle were the dockers, whose union, the DWR & GWU, provided a convenient umbrella for many workers in other trades, but in 1889 the gasworkers were equally important and equally successful in recruiting members in other industries.

Success, however, was short-lived, for by 1892 the employers had begun a counter-offensive which culminated in the Black Friday incident of December 1892, when a march of locked-out deal runners (dockers) and striking women confectionery workers was broken up by police and cavalry. By the spring of 1893 the deal runners and confectionery workers had been defeated and the membership of the general unions declined very quickly. Between the middle of the 1890s and 1910 the Dockers' Union in Bristol retained a foothold among the corn porters at the docks, but all other members had been lost, whilst the

This is probably one of the oldest photographs taken of Bristol Dockers. The original has faded very badly, but it has been included because of its great historic interest.

Gasworkers Union kept a base among the gasworkers, Corporation workers and some building labourers. Once again, the vast mass of unskilled workers lapsed into non-unionism.

National lock-outs of the miners in 1893 and of the boot and shoe workers in 1895 completed the rout of the unions. Both these unions had been involved in the events of 1889 in Bristol, but in the mid 1890s they were defeated and, in Kingswood, union organisation among boot and shoe workers disappeared completely. In coal-mining the union survived, but in 1910 it was estimated that 40% of the local coalminers did not belong to the union, the Bristol Miners Association (BMA). Only the craft unions in the building trade continued to make slow but steady progress, and where union organisation did survive among unskilled workers, this was dependent upon the continued recognition by employers. Such recognition was only granted on the understanding that the unions avoided militancy and pursued their aims through conciliation and arbitration.

Weakness, caution and moderation were thus the hallmarks of trades unionism in Bristol when our period opens in 1910. Yet within a year, the situation was being radically transformed as membership again increased and some unions were pushed, by the pressure of events, into adopting a more aggressive, militant posture. Indeed, much of the industrial scene in the years immediately preceding the outbreak of war in 1914 was disturbed by major confrontations between employers and workers, some on a national scale and increasingly involving the state. Bristol, like other major cities, was affected by these events.

The first signs of a revival of trade unionism among dockers in Bristol appeared in June 1910 when a dispute occurred at Avonmouth after the Houlders' Shipping Company diverted one of its ships there from the strikebound Newport docks. Union and non-union dockers at Avonmouth refused to work on the ship and when the Dockers union officials disowned the strikers they organised their own strike committee. Eventually a compromise was reached when the union officials intervened, but the dispute flared up again in July, by which time the employers had made extensive preparations, including the bringing in of trainloads of strike-breakers and a Shipping Federation Depot ship to accommodate them.

This resulted in the whole of the Avonmouth, Bristol and Portishead docks being brought to a standstill. The dispute attracted the attention of the Trades Council and socialist groups who formed a Docks Dispute Council to rally support for the dockers. By the end of the month, however, another compromise agreement had been reached and, although the Dockers' Union could not claim a victory, neither had it been defeated. (6)

Indeed, the Dockers' Union, despite the fact that its officials had at first been reluctant to support the stand of the Avonmouth dockers, made very significant gains during the following weeks and months. In August 1910,

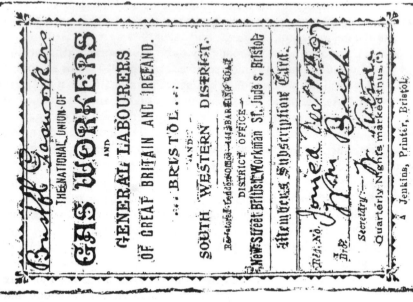

THE NATIONAL UNION OF

GAS WORKERS

AND

GENERAL LABOURERS

OF GREAT BRITAIN AND IRELAND.

...BRISTOL...

AND

SOUTH WESTERN DISTRICT.

Registered Head Office—143 Barking Road

DISTRICT OFFICE

New Street British Workman St. Jude's, Bristol

Members Subscription Card

Reg. No. James Leckham

Dr. to Wm Brick

Secretary:— R. Tubbs

Quarterly Nights marked thus (')

Jenkins, Printer, Bristol.

Quarter Nights the last Week, in March, June, September and December

Any Member not clearing the books on Quarter Night will be suspended until fourteen days after arrears are paid.

Any Member owing more than six weeks contributions will not be entitled for benefit.

NOTICE.

The Secretary will not be answering for any money paid without this card

Gas Workers union card 1897

2,000 new members were enrolled and this growth in membership continued into 1911. Of even greater significance was the broadening of the base of membership by the Dockers' Union which began with the establishment of the carters' branch, with Ernest Bevin its secretary. Bevin's declared reason for launching the branch was that during the docks dispute, carters had been called upon to help break the strike. (7)

The events of 1910 were but a mild foretaste of the explosion of militant trade union activity in the summer of 1911. In many ways the strikes of 1911 contained echoes of the events of 1889, involving many of the same groups of workers. The seamen were the first to stop work in Bristol, becoming involved in a national stoppage in early June. In July, when the seamen's strike was virtually over, there were several small disputes on the docks. In August, following the success of the London dock strike, the first ever national railway strike began. At the very same time the Bristol dockers and carters also stopped work; partly in sympathy with the railwaymen and partly in support of their own demands for increased wages. During the weekend of 19 - 20 August, the Western Daily Press reported that 'strike fever was at its height'. To counter the picketing of the railway goods yards, extra troops were moved into Horfield barracks and deployed at stations, goods depots and signal boxes. The most serious incident of the weekend occurred in Bedminster on the Saturday evening when troops fired over the heads of a crowd who were attacking a signal box. So seriously did the authorities view the situation that the Lord Mayor and J.P.s began to enrol volunteer special constables. (8)

By Monday, however, the railway strike had been settled and within a few days the dockers had achieved most of their demands. The strike by local coal miners, on the other hand, proved to be much more difficult to resolve. Beginning in August 1911, it dragged on until November before the miners returned to work, having gained only half the increase originally demanded. In March 1912 the miners were again involved in strike action when the Miners Federation of Great Britain declared a national strike in support of the demand for a national minimum wage, something which had a particular significance for a low-wage mining area like Bristol. Also in 1912 the dockers were again involved in strike action when, in June, they came out in sympathy with the London dock strike, although they returned to work again very quickly when it became clear that no other port would join the strike. (9)

The strikes which occurred in these years arose from diverse causes and can only be properly understood within the context of the particular circumstances of each of the industries involved. Yet there were also a number of common factors. The years 1909-1913 saw a rapid expansion in trade and industry and this was a time of rising expectations among many trade unionists. The period followed one in which real wages in general had fallen. Some commentators have also drawn attention to the dissatisfaction felt by many workers at the results of gaining the right to vote and of giving electoral support to the

Discharging stems of Jamaican bananas by hand at Avonmouth 1910

reformist political parties. This is often cited as one of the reasons for the growing influence of syndicalist ideas in areas like South Wales and Glasgow. As far as Bristol was concerned, no evidence has been found of any significant syndicalist influence in the strikes of 1910-1912, which appear to have been simply attempts by various groups of workers to recoup some of their losses, in terms of wages, conditions and trade union organisation, which they had suffered in the years preceding 1909. A possible indication of syndicalist influence is in the element of sympathetic strike action which was present, to a greater or lesser extent, in all three major dock strikes in 1910, 1911 and 1912; but there is no direct evidence of any sydicalist involvement in these events.

At first sight it might be tempting to view the strike of 1911-1912 as a repeat performance of the events of 1889-90. Both periods saw a rapid spread of strike action from one industrial centre to another and from industry to industry. The leading part played by dock workers was another common feature. In some places, notably in London and Liverpool, successful dock strikes sparked off waves of stoppages in other local industries, repeating the pattern of 1889. In Bristol, however, this was not the case. Strike action in Bristol during 1911-12 was almost entirely confined to the docks, road transport, the railways and the coal mining industry. The large numbers of workers in factories and small workshops, many of whom had been drawn into the 1889 struggles, were entirely absent from the events of 1911-12. The dockers did succeed in expanding their membership base but only into the carting trade, a closely related branch of the transport industry. As for the Gasworkers' Union, which had been prominent in 1889, there was no sign of a revival in its militancy in 1911.

The events of 1911-12, then, represented an attempt by particular groups of workers to obtain redress for particular grievances by a common resort to strike action. The results, which often fell far short of their expectations, led them to attempt to strengthen their trade union organisations.

Trade union organisation was increasing generally at this time. The Dockers' Union, for example, grew from a national membership of 18,000 in 1910 to one of 47,000 in 1914. (10) No accurate figures for the local membership of the Dockers' Union are available, but we can gain some insight into the size of its membership by studying the figures for income. In 1910, the Dockers' Union in Bristol had an income of £1,670; by 1911 this figure had increased to £3,704 and by 1914 the income was £3,723. (11) Among the 'general' unions, the Dockers' was by far the most successful in increasing its membership in the years 1910-14, although the other unions did make modest gains. Unions for skilled craftsmen, such as the Amalgamated Society of Engineers (ASE) (12) The Amalgamated Society of Carpenters and Joiners (ASCJ) (13) and the Operative Bricklayers Society (OBS) (14) also recorded increased membership in Bristol at this time, although their membership had been increasing steadily even before 1910. One exception to this rule of general growth was the NUBSO which did not begin to show an increased membership until after 1914. (15)

Despite its success, the Dockers' Union in Bristol remained essentially a union of dockers and road transport workers until 1914. Between 1910 and 1914 there was a drive to unionise the whole of the dock labour force and those in related trades. The *Dockers' Record* of March 1911 reported impressive progress:

> *The bargemen and lightermen have come along. The carmen are holding together well and at no distant date the branch will be 1,000 strong...The warehousemen are also joining the carters' branch and they are the last link in the chain. If the warehousemen come along, as it is expected they will, every section connected with dock and wharf work will be covered by the union.*

Thus the Dockers' Union succeeded in building up a position on the Bristol docks which was unique in waterfront trades unionism at that time. By 1913 it was able to claim a virtual monopoly of all grades and sections of dock workers, together with warehousemen and carters. Elsewhere it was common to find several unions vying with one another, and for waterfront trades unionism to be weakened as a result. In Bristol, by contrast, the Dockers' Union established a strong position. Bevin told the 1913 Annual Meeting of the National Transport Workers Federation that, in Bristol

> *it is a consciousness on the part of the employer the whole time he is negotiating with the coal-trimmer, the docker, carter, or seaman, that they have a combined executive behind them representing the co-operation of their fellows in the same organisation, that gives power to the negotiator...*
>
> *Where there is one union covering all the transport and the bulk of the general labourers in the town, what is the first thing the employers ask? It is, 'Will you all strike together?'* (16)

Unions generally tend to aim to achieve a monopoly position within their own industry, but for the dockworkers' unions this was particularly important as a means of protecting their members from the effects of the casual labour system by reducing competition for employment at the calling-on stands.

But the Dockers' Union could not provide such protection by recruiting dock workers alone since the numbers of men on the calling-on stands were frequently swelled by the unemployed and under-employed from other trades in the city. There was therefore an in-built tendency for the Dockers' Union to seek to extend its membership into other industries and trades.

H.A. Turner has also drawn attention to the 'institutional imperative' which forced general unions like the Dockers' and Gasworkers' to seek to

Registered Trade Union No. 483.

Reg. No....... *Weekly Contribution......*

Dock, Wharf, Riverside & General Workers' Union of Great Britain and Ireland.

General Sec.: BEN TILLETT, M.P

Now Amalgamated with the

Transport & General Workers' Union

Registered Office:

Effingham House, Arundel Street, STRAND, LONDON, W.C.2.

Branch Shop

B. 3

Name....................

Date of Joining..............

Occupation..............

Branch Secretary's Name & Address:

Mr. A. BIGNE.
9 .... St.
BRISTOL.

1.—Any member whose contributions exceed six weeks in arrears, shall not be entitled to benefit. Any member allowing his contributions to exceed six weeks in arrears shall serve probationary period of four weeks from date of bringing himself into compliance.

2.—It is the duty of the Branch Secretary to produce at each Branch Meeting the Central Office Receipt for the previous week's income. Members should see that this is complied with.

3.—No strike will be recognised unless ordered by the Executive Council.

T. W. GOUDGE, Printer, T.U., Plaistow.

An early T & GWU union card

NATIONAL UNION OF

RAILWAYMEN

England, Ireland, Scotland & Wales

HEAD OFFICE

Unity House, Euston Road, LONDON, N.W.

Member's Card for 19/6 to 19¾4

Bch. No. 399 ...H.O. No........

Bristol No. 6 Branch.

Member W. A. Baxter Eng. N.R.

Address Firs with Brislington

The Meetings of the Branch are held at Co-op. Hall, Brislington. Quarterly Meetings, March, June, September and December.

S. C. DAVIS, Branch Sec.,
39 Edward Road,
BRISLINGTON, BRISTOL.

PLEASE OBSERVE.

Any member owing more than thirteen weeks' contributions shall not be entitled to any of the benefits of the Union, but shall be entitled to receive benefits as soon as the paid his arrears; if owing more than sixteen weeks' contributions, he shall remain out of benefit until three months after the arrears are paid; should he owe more than twenty six weeks' contributions he shall cease to be a member, and thereby be expelled the Union Rule 2, Clause 10.

Members should observe that they are suspended from all benefits if dues and returns to Head Office are not made as required by Rule 10, Clause 11.

SICK FUND.

Contributions to the Sick Fund must be paid to Branch ... the other contributions to ...

A member ... are thirteen ... entitled to ... ... shall not again be ... ... ee months after his ... entitled to ... See Rule 17 Section 7 arrears are paid up ... ... Clause 9, Section 4, Clause 6.

—J. E. WILLIAMS Gen. Sec.

LET YOUR PRIDE BE A CLEAR CARD.

Bristol Printers Ltd Stratton Street

expand their membership. (17) He argues that such unions needed large numbers of members paying membership subscriptions to pay their relatively high costs of administration.

Before 1914 the Dockers' Union in Bristol had attempted to recruit members in the oil milling, flour milling and galvanising trades, with little initial success. The war, however, transformed the situation for trades unions, for the combined effects of full employment, rapid price inflation and growing food shortages, led growing numbers of workers to join unions. Moreover, the imposition of compulsory arbitration in industrial disputes forced all but the most recalcitrant of employers to recognise union negotiating rights. The increase in union membership during the war years was common to all unions. Thus the ASE, which in 1913 had a local membership of 1,095, had increased to 2,126 by 1917, and to 3,159 by 1919. NUBSO's success was even more remarkable: a membership of 1,268 in 1913 grew to 4,151 by 1917 and to 5,336 by 1919.

It was the Dockers' Union, however, which recorded the most striking increase. Accurate membership figures are not available but an indication of the union's success can be gained from figures for annual income for the Bristol district. A comparison with the Gasworkers' Union and the Workers' Union, the only other 'general' unions with a significant presence in the Bristol area, shows how far the Dockers' Union outstripped its rivals in the Bristol area, although nationally the picture was reversed.

Annual Income of selected general unions, Bristol district, 1910-1919.

Union	1910	1912	1914	1916	1918	1919
	£	£	£	£	£	£
DWR & GWU(18)	1,670	3,374	3,723	7,077	17,537	27,791
G & G LU(19)	116	350	630	620	3,000	3,750
WU(20)	78	114	199	181	1,111	1,924

The majority of the new recruits into the Dockers' Union during the war years were from the various factory and workshop trades of the city, including the confectionery industry, tobacco, aircraft manufacture, wagon-building, and the metal and chemical trades. Area branches were opened in Bristol East and Bristol South, staffed by their own full-time officials, to cope with what was described as 'a wave of unorganised workers to join our union'. Women workers made up a significant proportion of these new recruits, who were mainly unskilled workers. (21)

Unions like the Dockers' and Gasworkers' had always aspired to be 'general workers' unions yet, except for a brief period after their birth in the struggles of 1889, they had been unable to realise this. After 1917, however, general

Deal running in the City Docks about 1929. Each piece of timber was carried ashore on a man's shoulder. Often at the end of the working day men would find their skin torn and bleeding from constant rubbing by the wood.

worker members outnumbered the dockers and transport workers in the DWR & GWU. Why, however, should the majority of these workers have chosen the Dockers' Union in preference to other 'general' unions or, in some cases, an industrial union? Many of those who joined the Dockers' Union worked in factories which had connections with the docks as the point of entry of their raw materials.

Many of the factories had direct links with the docks through water-borne transport or road transport and the Dockers' Union was able to exploit these links. Thus in 1922 the local secretary of the Gasworkers Union complained that carters and drivers from firms where all workers, including themselves, were members of the G & MWU were unable to get goods unloaded at Bristol docks unless they transferred to the Dockers' Union. (22)

For the new members from the factory trades, membership of the Dockers' Union might have appeared to bring benefits in terms of enhanced bargaining power. Union officials were keen to stress this. Thus in 1921, one local official, using the tobacco industry as an example, sought to illustrate this point:

> *The tobacco arrives by ships and is handled by members of the T & GWU working in the hold of the ship...Secondly, it is conveyed from the dock-side to the tobacco warehouse by steam and motor wagons, the drivers of which are also our members. The tobacco has to be moved from warehouse to factory, still by members of the union. Our members also take part in the manufacture. Therefore, the workers, in the event of any attempt by the employers to do injustice to the factory workers, could, if necessary, have support from the whole of the other sections.* (23)

New recruits, therefore, could expect positive advantages to accrue from their membership of the Dockers' Union. The advantages to the union itself of expanding its membership into occupational groups, whose security and regularity of employment was far better than that of the dockers, have already been touched upon. There were also real, if perhaps less obvious, advantages for the dockers themselves, since the extension of union membership into the variety of transport and 'general' trades of the city enabled the union to achieve a position from which it could begin to regulate the competition for employment at the calling-on stands and so alleviate some of the worst effects of the casual labour system.

J. Lovell has pointed out that dock work was never as unskilled as has been thought. Indeed, many of the tasks undertaken by dock workers in the loading and unloading of ships required a relatively high level of skill and therefore required specialists to undertake them. (24)Because of the casual labour system and the lack of any formal apprenticeship system, however, dock workers were unable to control entry to their trade in the way that skilled craftsmen in other industries did. The result was a large reserve pool of under-employed dock labourers competing for work daily. The problem was exacerbated by the tendency of other groups of workers, such as those employed in road transport, the brickyards and even some of the factory and workshop trades, to seek employment at the docks when their own trades were depressed. These were the men whom Bevin described as the 'once-a-weekers'; they were not sufficiently skilled to undertake most dock work, but could be employed unloading the one banana boat which called at Avonmouth each week, or on other unskilled tasks. Unloading banana boats was not popular work with regular dockers and they were prepared, during periods of brisk trade to allow this to be done by truly casual workers; during periods of poor trade, however, regular dockers expected to be given preference over casual workers, for all the available employment.

Union officials in general, and Bevin in particular, consistently pressed the employers to decasualise dock work; but, before the war, there was very little progress. Once the Union had achieved a monopoly over union membership on the docks and begun to recruit the other transport and many of the 'general' workers of the city, it was in a position to begin to regulate the casual labour system through its own organisation. The first step was to ensure that those men who regularly sought work at the docks were given preference for employment, but the problem for the union was to differentiate between the 'regulars' and the 'casuals'. Bevin's solution, implemented in Bristol before 1914, was to divide union members into two categories - dock workers and general workers - and issue each with a different union membership certificate, or 'ticket'. It was then possible for union officials to check members' tickets at the calling - on stands and try to ensure preferential treatment for those holding a dockers' ticket.

During the war, decasualisation progressed even further. After the introduction of conscription in January 1916, regular dock workers were granted exemption from military service on the grounds that their occupation was essential to the war effort. [25] This privilege was not extended to casual dock workers, and the drawing up of a register of regular dockers thus became an urgent necessity. This was done under the auspices of a new Port Labour Committee, representing both the employers and the Union. Thus the Union's role in the regulation of dock labour and the process of decasualisation was officially recognised. The metal tallies which were issued to registered dockers were given out through the Union offices. After the war, whereas in other ports this scheme fell into disuse, registration continued in Bristol and dove-tailed neatly into Bevin's pre-war scheme for differentiating between regular and truly casual dock workers. Two types of tally were issued, one for regular dock workers and another for the carters and warehousemen and others who occassionally sought employment at the docks. This was of benefit to dockworkers but could also be of benefit to members of the union's general workers section. The *Dockers' Record* of February 1920 reported that members

March 30th. No. 3. Branch. T. Mayo
Officers. present A. Stone sec. g. May check sec.
C. Workman. door. keeper. with H. Tomkins in the chair
H. Hathrell. District Delagates absent through
ilness at Home Bro. Bevin was present and gave
a report. re. Invalidity + unemployment scheme
he stated That the letters had not been sent
to the members of Parliament up to the present
Because through obgation of the Dockers Union
and others Bodies Mr. L. George was forming a
scheme to include all grades of workman.
A. notice was read from head office Notefing members
to report all Accidents to branch sec. each meeting
night also stateing it has come to their knowledge that
men were settling sums for small sums when they should
get more a dussucion takpalace. to Hove open air meeting
Bro Bevin said he would speak on April 9. and
ask our gen sec. Ben Tillett to take the Chair this
closed the buisness for the evening.
Amount taken £ .H = 12 = 3.
W. Fry. Moved the minutes as read be correct
H. Hathrell second.
                Signed. H. Tomkins Chairman

Minutes of Branch No. 3 of the DWR & GWU held on March 30th 1911 of the Kingsley Hall, Bristol.

of the general workers' section who had been made redundant were finding casual employment unloading banana boats:

The average number is 250 per week, and special permits are given to the men through the union. The system of issuing tallies keeps the men entirely under the control of the organisation and avoids having hundreds of men fighting at the dock gates for employment.

The splitting of the membership into two categories of transport and general workers was the basis of the new union which emerged out of the amalgamation, in 1921, of the DWR & GWU with a number of smaller unions - the Transport and General Workers Union. Bevin was the architect of the organisational structure of the Union with its national trade groups superimposed upon a regional structure. The experience which he had gained as a trade union official in Bristol between 1910 and 1914 clearly influenced Bevin's thinking on this. The dock workers occupied a key position in the new Union, just as they had within the DWR & GWU. They were the original membership group and the one whose particular needs and problems had most exercised the energies of the Union's officials. In many ways the splitting of the membership into separate transport and general workers sections arose as a response to the particular problems of dock workers.

Yet it also catered for the sectional interests of many other groups who had been recruited by the Union and who might have been in danger of being submerged within a vast organisation like the T&GWU. Indeed, the trade group solution had already been adopted on an ad hoc basis before 1921 in other areas. The Dockers' Union's members in the South Wales tinplate industry, for example, had been organised into a separate trade group before 1914. (26) Such a solution enabled each trade group to enjoy considerable autonomy within the overall policy-making structure of the union and to employ officials who specialised in negotiations within a single industry or a set of related industries. Moreover, it was a strategy which enabled the Union to present itself, at one and the same time, as a union which embraced wide sections of the working class and as a union which catered for the sectional interests and often the status-consciousness of different groups of workers. Thus the clerical workers' section was able to present itself as a separate union within a union by adopting its own name, the Association of Clerical, Technical and Supervisory Staffs, and frequently to recruit white collar workers from the same firms as those in which the Union had manual worker members.

The trade group structure introduced by Bevin was an ingenious device to accommodate sectional interests within a wide-ranging amalgamation of workers from different industries, with different levels of skill, status and responsibility. This entrenchment of sectionalism within the Union's structure was a far cry from the original aims of the founders of the Union, which were: to build a general union fighting for class-wide, socialist aims, as well as for the immediate objectives of particular groups of workers. Bevin undoubtedly regarded his union structure as a realistic response to the circumstances of a time when large numbers of workers were joining unions of all types, primarily in order to seek redress for their own particular grievances. The T & GWU, like the Dockers' Union before it, was in competition with well-established industrial unions in a number of industries and needed to show its ability to cater separately for each new group of recruits. On the other hand, many workers, joined the Dockers' Union and its successor the T & GWU, precisely because it was a large amalgamation with greater resources and because of the enhanced bargaining power which might result from having dockers and road transport workers as fellow members. In other words, it was at least possible that some of those who joined the DWR & GWU (T & GWU) looked to the possibility of active links with other sections of members, if only to strengthen their own hand in negotiations with their own employers.

Reports in the union journal, the *Dockers' Record*, suggest that union officials may well have encouraged potential members to believe that they could expect the support of the dockers if they should find themselves in dispute with their employers. The number of occasions when sympathetic strike action by dockers did occur were very few, but there is some evidence that Bristol dockers were prepared to show solidarity with other groups of workers. The 1910 docks dispute had occurred when Bristol dockers showed their solidarity with striking dockworkers in Newport by refusing to unload a ship transferred from there. In 1912 the Bristol dockers were the only ones in the country to respond to the NTWF's (National Transport Workers Federation) appeal to all dockers to strike in support of the London dock strike. Such solidarity, moreover, was not only shown towards other dockworkers. In 1911 one of the reasons for the stoppage on the Bristol and Avonmouth docks was to show support for striking railwaymen, although the dockers also had their own grievances. In the following year, one local branch of the DWR & GWR called upon the NTWF to declare a national transport strike in support of the miners' minimum-wage strike (27)

1913 and 1914 were relatively quiet years in Bristol industry, but elsewhere there were major confrontations - in the cornish China Clay industry and in Dublin. Here again, Bristol dockers showed their sympathy by making collections towards the strike funds and expressing moral support through large trade union gatherings.

It is not being suggested that Bristol dockers were prepared to strike at every opportunity, nor that they submerged their sectional aims within a wider class-consciousness. Yet there seems to have been among many Bristol dockers, in the years before World War I, a growing interest in and sympathy with the problems of other groups of workers, whether in the same or in different industries, and this occasionally manifesed itself in sympathetic strike action.

This tension between sectionalism and a more generalised trade unionism, or even class-consciousness, was clearly apparent in the Triple Industrial Alliance. Established in 1914, this was an alliance of miners, railwaymen and transport workers which aimed to strengthen the hands of each of these key groups in their dealings with employers and governments. When its formation was announced it was celebrated in Bristol by what the *WDP* described as 'one of the greatest labour demonstrations organised locally'.(28) Bristol was well placed to organise such a demonstration for it was one of the few industrial centres where all the occupational groups involved lived in close proximity to one another. Because of this, Bristol provides a useful vantage point from which to study rank and file trades unionists' attitudes towards the Alliance.

The obviously enthusiastic support from all three sections from the Triple Alliance demonstration in July 1914 suggests that there was a growing sense of trade union solidarity. Dockers in Bristol had already shown this solidarity in a number of ways, whilst railwaymen and miners had both been involved in major conflicts where the support of the other groups of workers had proved to have been of value.

Recent studies, however, have shown that the Triple Alliance at national level was an organisation through which the member unions sought to press their sectional claims even more strongly, rather than submerge them in a common struggle for greater social justice. (29) Union leaderships, moreover, were unwilling to sacrifice their autonomy in making policy decisions in favour of a common Alliance policy. Thus, at its first major test in 1921, when the miners called on the other unions to help them resist wage cuts, the Alliance collapsed. The leaders of the railwaymen and the transport workers failed to organise support from their members for the miners and the miners were left to fight on alone.

It may be tempting to regard sectionalism as having been the policy of trade union officials, and the idea of trade union solidarity as having come from the rank and file. Such an interpretation would be far too simplistic. Although sectionlism can be seen to have become enshrined in the organisational structures of unions, even of 'general' unions such as the DWR & GWU (T & GWU) it has its roots in the experiences and aspirations of rank and file trade unionists. For the most part, workers joined a trade union because they regarded it as a possible vehicle for the redress of their own particular grievances. Whilst they might choose to join a union like the DWR & GWR which offered the prospect of support from other key groups of workers like the dockers, their motives for joining at all were almost entirely to do with sectional grievances rather than class-wide aspirations.

Many trade union officials, for their part, frequently used the language of class conflict, especially during the immediate pre-war years and in the years 1919-1926. Bevin, for example, constantly referred to class differences and was

Royal Edward Dock, warehouses, Avonmouth. Reception of goods from ship's side by electric truck. 1926

even to be found, during 1913 and 1914 at public meetings in Bristol, advocating a general strike. (30) Within the trade union structures there appears to have been some difference in attitude between local and national officials. In 1921 after the Black Friday fiasco, for example, local officials in Bristol criticised their national leaders for their failure to stand by the miners.

It is at least possible, therefore that many union officials were able to take a broader view of the struggles in which their unions were involved than their members. Neverthless, there is some evidence from the immediate post-war in Bristol that many rank and file trades unionists were prepared to go further in demonstrating solidarity with each other than their union executives believed to be either possible or desirable. During the miners' strike of 1920 local railwaymen held a mass meeting to pledge support for any sympathy action the Alliance might take. (31) In the following year, railwaymen again pledged themselves to take strike action in support of the miners and a local committee of Triple Alliance unions was formed to co-ordinate action locally. (32) When the strike was called off, a large mass meeting of Triple Alliance unions was highly critical of the executives, although the decision not to strike in support of the miners was obeyed. In May 1921, however, Bristol dockers brought the port to a standstill over their refusal to work on a ship which was burning German coal. After the intervention of union officials, however, the strike was called off. (33)

One of the main concerns of union officials, in seeking to limit the participation of their members in sympathetic strikes, seems to have been their desire to protect their negotiating machinery. They clearly perceived the threat that employers might withdraw recognition from the unions and abandon the negotiating machinery if union members stopped work in support of other workers rather than in furtherance of a trade dispute of their own. Much of the work of union officials was in negotiating the rules governing the working conditions of their members and in resolving the disputes which arose from the application of those rules. Local agreements reached between the Dockers' Union and the various docks employers in this period reveal a complex web of rules and regulations governing manning levels, the use of machinery, piece rates etc, which had been arrived at by negotiation and which gave rise to frequent disputes over their interpretation.

In order for union officials to render a continual service to their members, such agreements were essential as were the procedural agreements for resolving disputes. Procedure agreements were becoming more common and were increasing in complexity during these years.

From an employer's point of view, collective bargaining implied a loss of managerial prerogative, and many employers continued to refuse recognition to unions. Involvement in collective bargaining, however, conferred on the employer the advantage of committing union officials to rules and procedures which had been agreed jointly and which the officials were expected to ensure

Weigher on ship's deck making bags up to exact weight in buyer's sacks for purchases. 1922.

were honoured by their members. In other words, through collective bargaining, union officials increasingly took on the role of managers of conflict, policing the agreements which they had reached with employers, and attempting to channel disputes through agreed procedures. Such a commitment undoubtedly weighed heavily on the minds of many union officials at times when sympathetic strike action was being considered.

Yet this tendency towards the institutionalisation of conflict was not the only pressure on trade union officials at this time and it would clearly be a mistaken view to regard them as having been drawn inevitably into the role of 'managers of discontent'. Nor should it be assumed that union officials automatically lost sight of the wider aims of the labour movement, in the way that R. Michels has suggested. (34) In a situation of increasing industrial conflict and sharpening class tensions, such as existed immediately before and in the years after World War I, union leaders inevitably found themselves leading their members into battle. The machinery of collective bargaining, conciliation and arbitration was placed under severe strain.

Thus in 1912, when Bristol dockers stopped work in sympathy with the London dock strikers, the strike was called off after three days when Bristol employers took out summonses against 200 carters for alleged breach of contract and demanded that their employees leave the union. This was not the only factor in the calling off of the sympathy action - the failure of dockers elsewhere to respond in like manner was undoubtedly a crucial factor - but the incident does serve to demonstrate the rather ambivalent attitude of Dockers' Union officials to sympathetic strike action.

This ambivalence was again demonstrated during the Black Friday crisis of 1921 and during the General Strike of 1926. In 1926, when the miners faced a demand for wage reductions and increased hours, the trade unions responded on a much broader front - the action being co-ordinated by the TUC rather than the, by then, defunct Triple Alliance. In Bristol, on 3 May 1926, there seems to have been a willing and enthusiastic response to the TUC's call for a general strike. The miners had already been locked out on 1 May. They were joined at midnight on 3 May by the dockers, railwaymen, road transport and building workers and, within the next few days, by printing workers, electrical power station workers and engineers. As the strike went on the numbers involved increased so that on 12 May when the strike was called off, there were an estimated 36, 000 workers on strike in Bristol and there seems to have been no significant return to work in any industry before this date. (35)

The strike committee did fail, however, to persuade the printworkers on the local newspapers or the tramway workers to join the strike. Meanwhile the flood of volunteers who enrolled for strike-breaking duty - an estimated 8,000 in all - were put to work on the docks, driving lorries, and on the railways. Sailors from the two warships which were sent in to Avonmouth and Bristol docks were employed in the docks, and in the electricity power station. As far as the strikers were concerned, however, there was no evidence of any serious weakening before 12 May, and the news that the strike had been called off by the TUC was met with considerable confusion. When it became clear that the TUC leaders had called off the strike without securing any concessions and had left the miners to fight on alone, the mood changed to one of anger. The numbers on strike, in fact, were higher in the days immediately after 12 May than before, but inevitably the strike collapsed and officials of each of the unions made the best arrangements they could to secure the return to work of their members.

A discussion of the reasons why the national officials of the unions should have called off the General Strike so precipitately, and without securing any concessions, does not belong in a local study of this kind. As far as Bristol was concerned the strike was not weakening before 12 May. After the defeat of the strike, however, trade unionism in Bristol was severely weakened. The combined effects of the defeat and mass unemployment reduced trade union membership drastically and forced the unions to adopt a cautious, defensive non-militant posture in the coming years. Between 1926 and 1939 there were hardly any strikes reported in Bristol.

Any further sympathetic strike action was made impossible by the defeat of the General Strike. For union members in many industries, indeed, the idea had not appeared feasible even before 1926. The boot and shoe workers, tailors and garment workers, furniture workers and those in large factories producing chocolate and cigarettes, for example, continued to conduct their industrial relations in almost complete isolation from the rest of the labour movement. In some cases, as with the confectionery and tobacco workers, wages and conditions tended to be better than average for Bristol; but wages and conditions in parts of the boot and shoe industry for example, were in many ways comparable with those of the miners. Yet the struggles of the boot and shoe workers to establish their union in Bristol and Kingswood and improve their conditions attracted very little attention, and still less support from the rest of the labour movement. They on their side appear to have played very little part in the trades council or to have involved themselves in the wider struggles of the labour movement. Other groups of workers, such as engineers, building workers and printing workers, only became involved in sympathetic action during the General Strike of 1926.

For the most part, then, it was the three groups of workers involved in the Triple Alliance of 1914 who showed most interest in other workers' struggles and, of these, it was the dockers who showed the greatest willingness to take sympathetic strike action. This partly reflects the importance of the docks, and the men employed there, within the local economy ; it also reflects the strong union organisation built up in the Bristol and Avonmouth docks between 1910 and 1914, which served as a base for extending union organisation into other industries during World War I. Perhaps, also, it stemmed from the tendency

Dockers at work on a cargo ship in Avonmouth, 1920.

among dockers when they themselves were involved in major strikes, a tendency observed in 1889 and again in 1911, to seek to enlist public support as a means of raising money and as a means of putting pressure on employers. By demonstrating solidarity with other workers when they were involved in struggles, the dockers may simply have been repaying a debt.

Postscript

The history of trades unionism in Bristol is long and complex and it would be impossible, within the limits of this article, to do that story justice (if an attempt were made to write a comprehensive account). Indeed, such a task could not yet be attempted since, although a considerable amount of research had already been done, many aspects of the history have not yet been investigated. Sadly there will always be gaps in our knowledge because of the lack of documentary evidence, much of which has disappeared for ever due to neglect and to the desruction during the last war. The historian who attempts to reconstruct and analyse trade union history in a city like Bristol has to work from incomplete primary sources and is forced to rely heavily on the local press and the unions' central records. These sources, however, inevitably present a distorted picture of trade union activities, since both tend to report the news of local and national trade union officials, whilst the attitudes and views of rank and file trade union members are very rarely reported.

---

(1)   Census of England and Wales, 1911
(2)   Census Reports, 1921 and 1931
(3)   NAFTA *Monthly Reports*
(4)   NUBSO *Monthly Reports*
(5)   S. Bryher *A History of the Labour and Socialist Movement in Bristol*
(6)   *Western Daily Press*, 22 - 28 June 1910; 13 - 23 July 1910.
(7)   *Dockers' Record* 1910 - 1911
(8)   *WDP* 21 August 1911
(9)   *WDP* 12 June 1912
(10)   GDH Cole, *Trade Unionism and Munitions* (1923), p. 197
(11)   DWR & GWU *Annual Reports, passim.*
(12)   ASE *Monthly Reports, passim*
(13)   ASCJ *Monthly Reports, passim*
(14)   OBS *Monthly Reports, passim*
(15)   NUBSO *Monthly Reports, passim*
(16)   Quoted in A. Bullock *The Life and Time of Ernest Bevin*, vol I p.40
(17)   H.A. Turner *Trade Union Growth, Structure and Policy* (1962)
(18)   DWR & GWU *Annual Reports, passim*
(19)   G & GLU *Quarterly Reports, passim*
(20)   WU *Annual Reports, passim*
(21)   *Dockers' Record* 1916 - 1919 *passim*
(22)   NUGW Biennial Congress, *Report*, 1922

(23) *The Record*, August 1921
(24) J. Lovell *Stevedores and Dockers* (1969)
(25) Hamilton Whyte, *The Decasualisation of Dock Labour* (Bristol 1934).
(26) E.J. Hobsbawm, General Labour Unions, 1889-1914; in: *Labouring Men* (1964)
(27) Bristol City Record Office, Minute Book, DWR & GWU No 3 Branch, 1911-17
(28) *WDP 25 November 1913*
(29) *P.S. Bagwell, The Triple Industrial Alliance 1913-22, in : Briggs and Saville ed, Essays in Labour History* Vol II (1971)
(30) *WDP 25 November 1913*
(31) BTM 20 October 1920
(32) *WDP 4 April 1921*
(33) *WDP 3 - 4 May 1921*
(34) *R. Michels, Political Parties*
(35) *WDP 1 - 13 May 1926, passim; BTM ibid.*

Bristol Women in Action, 1839 - 1919:
The right to vote and the need to earn a living.

Ellen Malos

Until very recently our ideas about participation by women in political and industrial action have been dominated by spectacular images of window smashing and forced feeding during the few short years of suffragette attacks on property. It is remembered as largely London-centred and focussed on a few famous individuals leading an anonymous mass. With the exception of a few isolated strikes, like the matchgirls' strike, again in London, movements for women's rights are thought of as an almost purely middle-class movement for the vote and nothing but the vote, directed at the Houses of Parliament.

It is now clear that women played an active part in political movements and activities from the late eighteenth century. They were involved in the Radical Reform movement that led up to Peterloo [1] in 1819 and in the Chartist movements [2] for working-class political rights and parliamentary reform in the 1830s and 40s, in small towns and villages throughout the country as well as in the large cities. [3] Women were active Chartists in Cheltenham, Trowbridge, Bath and Bristol as well as in other more spontaneous political activities such as food riots. [4]

Political activity by working-class women seems to have lessened in the middle of the nineteenth century. [5] But we now know that working-class as well as middle-class women worked for women's suffrage down the long years of campaigning for the extension of the right to vote until it finally covered all adults in 1928. Despite the vast gulfs and conflicting interests that lay between the different classes, middle-class as well as working-class women were also campaigning for the right of women to earn a decent living by their work and for their right to combine in unions. [6]

Bristol, the largest city in the area, was an important centre for women's movements in the South West. [7] The idea of women's political organisation in Bristol and the West County has been treated as a joke by some historians. In John Cannon's study of the Chartists in Bristol he dismisses the Female Patriotic Association as one of the 'peculiarly unconvincing...devices to which the Chartists now resorted in their search for support' after the arrest of Henry Vincent, the Chartist leader, in 1839.[8]

In contrast Dorothy Thompson [9] describes the strength of Chartism among women in West Country towns and villages, including Cheltenham, Trowbridge and Bath. On his 1837-8 tour of England, Henry Vincent described a meeting for women he spoke at, chaired by Mrs Bolwell, a local Chartist organiser, in Larkenhall Gardens in October, 1838:

Yesterday afternoon the whole road leading to the place of meeting was crowded by highly respectable females, some on foot and others in coaches and various vehicles wending their way to the place of meeting - the gardens which will hold at least 5,000 were crammed to suffocation - no males allowed within except Mr Kissock...Mr Young...and myself. There were hundreds outside who could not get near the place.

The Chartist demand for universal suffrage was ambiguous. Were women to be included, especially married women? (10) (Even many women's suffragists were later to be unsure about them.) At least some Chartist pamphlets argued that the vote ought to be extended to women and large numbers of women supported the Charter and the demand for the vote. There is no reason to suppose that their support was any weaker in Bristol than in the surrounding area. Although there seem to be no surviving local records of the activities of the Bristol Female Patriotic Association, contemporary newspaper accounts of Chartist meetings on Brandon Hill describe large audiences of both women and men for the Chartist speakers in the late thirties and early forties. (Women were also prominent in the Bristol riots in 1831.)

The direct political activity of both middle-class and working-class women was hindered by the spreading of the idea that a woman's place was in the home and the indifference or hostility of much of the organised Trade Union movement. This was especially so after the 1832 reform bill had given the male middle-class the parliamentary franchise, and the Chartist movement had been defeated. (11) But middle-class women of radical sympathies do seem to have had some form of organised association in Bristol.

A Bristol and Clifton Auxiliary Ladies Anti-Slavery Society was formed at a meeting in the Temperance Hotel, Bath Street, on 17 September, 1840. The Society consistently supported the radical abolitionists in the United States from the 1850s on. (12) At this time the British Anti-Slavery movement was divided both on the future direction of actions against slavery and on whether women should be eligible, as before, to act on the committee of the Anti-Slavery Society and to vote on its policies. (13)

A number of women who became active in the Bristol and Clifton Society for Women's Suffrage after it was formed in 1868 were committee members of this society. In the early Fifties the Ladies Society disaffiliated from the British and Foreign Anti-Slavery Society because of the latter's anti-radical stance and a correspondence was developed with radical abolitionists in America and particularly with the women who became active in the American Civil Rights movement.

Mary Estlin joined the committee of the Ladies Anti-Slavery Society in 1851, later becoming Treasurer of the Women's Suffrage Society. She corresponded with abolitionists and Women's Rights supporters in the United States and met such women as Lucretia Mott, Elizabeth Cady Stanton, Sarah

REPORT

OF THE

𝔅ristol & 𝔚est of 𝔈ngland 𝔖ociety

FOR

WOMEN'S SUFFRAGE,

1873.

OBJECT.—To obtain for Women Householders and Ratepayers the right of Voting for Members of Parliament.

BRISTOL:
H. HILL, STEAM PRINTER, 2 BALDWIN STREET.

1874.

Grimke, Lucy Stone, Susan B. Anthony and other prominent members of the American Women's Rights movement on a visit there in 1868. On her return to Bristol she sent her friend Sarah Pugh pamphlets and essays from Britain, including Professor Francis Henry Newman's published lectures on Women's Suffrage for the newly formed Bristol Society. (14) In 1883 Elizabeth Cady Stanton visited Bristol as a friend of the Estlins and addressed the new Women's Liberal Association, the first in the country.(15) The Winkworth and Priestman sisters of Bristol had already been involved in the signing of the petition for Women's Suffrage presented to Parliament by John Stuart Mill in 1866 and in informal meetings in Manchester to organise the campaign during 1867. (16)

The society was formed at a meeting by invitation at the home of Commissioner Davenport Hill at 3 The Mall, Clifton, on 24 January 1868. The invitation, in a circular from Professor Newman, stated that Mr Commissioner Hill (17) 'permits his daughter Miss Florence Davenport Hill to issue it', (18) an indication of the difficulty that middle-class Victorian women had in breaking out of the patriarchal cocoon.

The 1867 Reform Act had extended the Parliamentary vote to all male ratepayers in the towns and Jacob Bright's amendment, granting the municipal franchise to women on the same terms as men, had already been passed by Parliament. Those who attended the meeting had no idea of the long struggle before women would gain the parliamentary franchise.

The object of the campaign was to get women who seemed to be qualified for the vote as ratepayers to register, because the act did not specify 'male persons' and one woman had voted in a bye-election in Manchester in 1867 (19) - but hopes were soon dashed.

Mrs Beddoe, a member of the first committee, described the first meeting:

> *I had been very ill but was out again in a bath chair when I received an invitation from Mr Commissioner Hill…to a meeting at his house… I found a large party of the fashionable part of the community present. He explained to us that the Society, which he wished to form, was unlike most others for it would require neither time nor money (a general smile), it was so evidently fair and just too - that it only required to be properly brought before parliament to be granted.*
> *Then the time came to sign and seal. In a few minutes the audience had disappeared as quickly as a flight of birds, leaving only myself (who was lame) and Mrs Goodeve, a lady so kind hearted that she would not have left anyone in the lurch. (20)*

The 'fashionable part of the community' appears to have been more curious than interested, but the movement quickly developed strength, especially from Quakers, Unitarians and other non-conformist religious groups, and

Radical Liberals. By 1871 and 1872 its listed sponsors included such people as Mary Carpenter, her nephew and biographer the Rev. J. Estlin Carpenter, and Dr Eliza Walker Dunbar, Bristol's first woman doctor, (21) as well as women and men from prominent landowning, manufacturing and professsional families throughout Somerset, Gloucester, Wiltshire and South Wales. By this time it had become the Bristol and West of England Branch of the National Society for Women's Suffrage. Many of those who were active in the movement had personal and family connections with other reform movements (e.g. the Anti-Corn Law League) in London and the Midlands as well as in Bristol.(22) Lilias Ashworth of Bath and Mrs W.S. Clark of Street were members of the same family as John and Jacob Bright and one of the Priestman sisters married into it. The women of both the Birmingham and Bristol branches of the Sturge family were also among the active members of the movement.

Lists of the Society's prominent members and sponsors, sometimes running to over fifty names, were published in the Annual reports. We do not know who the women were who attended the public and 'drawing room' meetings, (which in 1880 alone were held in the Charlton Hall, Lawrence Hill, the Temperance Hall, Bedminster, St Mark's Schoolrooms, Easton, the Colston Hall, and others in Central Bristol, and the Broadmead rooms, as well as in Stapleton, Clifton, Redland, and Cotham; meetings were also held in various towns in North and South Wales, Cornwall, Devon, and Gloucestershire). We do know that the meetings were large. A newspaper report quoted by Mrs Beddoe of a meeting in Bath on 22 April 1884, after listing the prominent citizens present (including the Mayor of Bath who was in the Chair), goes on to say that 'there were also many working women and a large attendance of men'.(23)

Both Mrs Beddoe and Lilias Ashworth Hallett wrote brief accounts of the early speaking tours the society organised. The first was in the spring of 1871, with Millicent Fawcett as speaker at Bath, Bristol, Exeter, Taunton, Plymouth and Tavistock, and another was the tour of Rhoda and Agnes Garrett (24) in 1872 in Gloucestershire and Wales. These early speaking tours must have taken a great deal of courage because it was still widely thought to be unwomanly and sensational for a woman to address a public meeting, particularly one with men present - though it did have the side effect of increasing the audience. Lilias Ashworth Hallett described these early meetings:

> *The novelty of hearing women speakers brought crowds to the meetings. Invariably the doors were thronged with people unable to obtain seats. The tours of meetings, consisting of six or seven in a fortnight were a great nervous effort in those early days. They were, however, a source of much interest, and even pleasure in the retrospect, for we never failed to*

carry our resolutions affirming the principle of the suffrage and adopting petitions to Parliament. Occasionally an amendment would be moved, but nowhere was it ever carried... Looking through a file of old newspapers, I see these comments:-

'The room was densely crowded - drawn thither by the announcement that feminine man, viz. three ladies, were to fight the cause. This they did right manfully, yet, withal, in a most clear, lucid and persuasive manner, without the least vulgarism.'

'Few ladies have courage Amazonian enough to brave the publicity of meeting.' At one meeting a clergyman arose and said, 'It was forbidden in Holy Scripture for women to speak or take part in public affairs'. After a heated discussion, a gentleman arose and said that his grandmother was a Quakeress and spoke constantly in Quaker churches, adding, 'Let anyone prove, who can, that she transgressed the laws of God or man'. A resolution for thanks to the Ladies was passed 'for their **heroism** *in giving such able and interesting speeches'.*

Another paper says: 'Whether we agree or not, we admire the courage of the ladies, who have given an intellectual treat'. (25)

Other reactions were not so tolerant. When Viscountess Amberley, another Bristol and West of England member, read a paper on women's suffrage at the Mechanics Institute at Stroud, the news angered Queen Victoria, causing her to make her much quoted remarks against 'this mad, wicked folly of "Women's Rights" with all its attendant horrors, on which her poor feeble sex is bent, forgetting every sense of womanly feelings and propriety'. The Queen, expressing her own womanly feelings, said that 'Lady Amberley ought to get a good whipping'. (26)

Activity in favour of a series of private bills to admit women to the suffrage on the same terms as men was intense during the 1870s and 1880s, especially in the period leading up to the Third Reform Bill, which gave the vote to County ratepayers in 1884. The annual reports of the Bristol and West of England Society list an almost endless series of large meetings and thousands of signatures collected for petition after petition throughout the West Country. The Report of 1880 describes one public meeting in the Colston Hall:

Probably the most remarkable meeting ever held in Bristol was that which took place on the 4th November last when the Colston hall was crowded by women, earnest and anxious to hear what women had to tell them of the questions connected with their political emancipation. The chair was taken by Mrs Beddoe, and when she entered the hall, followed by ladies who had assembled from all parts of the country as delegates to the meeting, no vacant place could be seen. The whole area and galleries of the hall were filled by thousands of women who received with enthusiasm the President and speakers as they came forward to address them. A large number who were unable to find access to the Great Hall assembled in the Arch Room below, where Miss Colman was called to the chair, the proceedings being similar to those in the larger meeting.

The meeting passed a women's suffrage resolution and a memorial to Mr Gladstone protesting against the exclusion of women ratepayers on the grounds that 'the exclusion of women ratepayers from the exercise of the parliamentary vote deprives women of that free exercise of opinion which is the only guarantee of liberty in the state'.

Though the inclusion of women ratepayers was a limited aim, it was not necessarily a conservative one, nor did it mean that those who supported it wanted to limit the extension of the vote to middle-and upper-class women. For some, at least, the bland phrases of the memorial to Gladstone translated itself into something more challenging: 'Taxation without representation is tyranny was our watchword then, and it is so now', wrote Mrs Beddoe in 1911. Anne and Mary Priestman translated the watchword into action in the 1870s by refusing to pay their taxes (27) and saw their dining room chairs and other articles seized and put up for auction by the authorities to raise the sum they had refused to pay.

The years from 1880 to 1884 were the peak of the early suffrage movement. The annual reports of the Bristol and West of England Society between 1882 and 1890 are missing from the files in the Fawcett library, but Mrs Beddoe wrote of the efficient organisation of many meetings throughout the West Country in those years. Helen Blackburn, the organiser of the meetings, was Joint Secretary of the Bristol and West of England Society and the National Society, dividing her time between Bristol and London.

A letter and poem sent to the Bristol Mercury by Maria Colby in 1883 refers to women's suffrage meetings on the Downs on 'twenty-two evenings successively' which she had organised, and contains her reply in verse to one of the recurring stock responses to the idea of women venturing beyond the family circle:

WOMAN'S MISSION.

To the Editor of the Bristol Mercury.

SIR,—As organising agent for the Women's Suffrage Meetings on the Downs, will you allow me to say that the objections to our claims, based on the idea that the primary duty of woman is to darn stockings, has been advanced about ten times a night for twenty-two evenings successively. Under these circumstances may it not be worth while to insert the following, for which if you will kindly find a corner you will oblige a multitude of ladies who desire to express their disapprobation of this theory, and their intense weariness of hearing it so often ventilated :—

Wanted—

A postman to marry, who walks with might,
Or policeman on duty by day and night,
Or telegraph racer with heels of horn,
Who'll bring me in daily some stockings to darn !
Stockings to wear, stockings to tear !
They'll take more husbands than I can bear.
I have mended at leisure twelve socks per day ;
Might manage four dozen, I'm proud to say.
Twelve husbands with stockings in boot and shoe
Won't give my needle enough to do.
Has anyone got a few husbands to spare,
Who have nothing to do but stockings to wear ?
Can Birmingham make them ?   Will Isle of man
Turn out some husbands as quick as it can !
My needle is idle, oh sad repose !
Must marry a wire-worm covered with toes !

Reflection—

Husbands and stockings to tend and mend ;
Sad tax on one's patience, and time no end.
Alas ! in the stock I can't take a share ;
'Twill cost more money than I can spare !
But truly, if woman's one aim in life
Is to be to stockings a faithful wife,
Let her choose some stockings from husbands free !
What darnless and beautiful socks they'll be !

Yours truly,

M. COLBY, Clifton (1883).

The years from 1869 to 1883 also involved many women in the campaign against the Contagious Diseases Acts, which applied to certain garrison towns and naval ports initially, though there was a possibility that they might be extended throughout the country. These Acts, the first of which was passed in 1864 and which were extended in 1869, were designed to protect soldiers and sailors against venereal disease. They laid down that a woman could be declared a common prostitute if a police inspector or superintendent or a medical man informed a magistrate that he believed her to be one. She then had to present herself for compulsory medical inspection and if found to be infected was to be immediately detained in a 'lock Hospital' for up to three months. Treatment with mercury, a poison, was the standard cure. (28)

The National Campaign Against the Contagious Diseases Acts was

BRISTOL AND WEST OF ENGLAND SOCIETY FOR WOMEN'S SUFFRAGE.

SUBSCRIPTIONS AND DONATIONS

1893 AND 1894.

	1893.				1894.		
	£	s.	d.		£	s.	d.
Hon. Mrs. Holmes a'Court	0	2	6	...			
Miss Avery	0	2	6	...	0	2	6
Miss Beddoe...	0	5	0	...	0	5	0
,, (donation)				...	1	0	0
Mrs. Beddoe				...	1	0	0
Mrs. Benjamin	0	10	6				
Mrs. Bagnall-Oakeley				...	0	10	0
Mrs. W. H. Budgett (donation) ...	1	1	0	...			
Lady Bowring	0	10	0	...			
Miss Butler	0	10	0	...	0	10	0
Miss Bulkley				...	0	2	6
Mrs. Clinker	0	2	6	...			
Miss Cocks	0	5	0	...			
Mr. John Cory	1	1	0	...			
Mrs. Croggan	0	5	0	...			
Miss Dahl	0	2	6	...	0	2	6
Dr. Eliza W. Dunbar	1	0	0	...	1	1	0
Mr. Dyke	0	2	0	...			
Miss de Ridder	0	5	0	...			
Miss Estlin	1	1	0	...			
Mrs. Rutherford-Elliot				...	0	5	0
Mrs. Sparke Evans	1	1	0	...	1	0	0
Mrs. Garnett (donation)	3	0	0	...			
Mrs. Hale	1	1	0	...	1	1	0
Mrs. Hallett	20	0	0	...	20	0	0
Mr. Hallett				...	5	0	0
Per Mrs. Hallett (Expenses of Bath Meeting)				...	9	6	0
Mrs. Harle	0	5	0	...	0	5	0
Miss F. Davenport Hill	0	2	6	...	0	2	6
Miss Hayward	0	5	0	...			
Mr. John Harvey	1	1	0	...			

launched from Bristol in September 1869 on the occasion of the British Social Science Congress at the Victoria Rooms. The Ladies National Committee Against the Acts, which organised independently under Josephine Butler, had very strong support in Bristol. In her *Personal Reminiscences of a Great Crusade*, written in 1898, Josephine Butler remembered particularly the Bristol group which still continued 'full of life and vigour':

> *I refer especially to the sisters Priestman and Margaret Tanner, with Miss Estlin and others closely associated with them who have been to me personally, through this long struggle, from the first years till now, a kind of bodyguard, a 'corps d'elite' on whose prompt aid, singleness of purpose, prudence and unwearying industry I could and can rely on at all times...(p 104-5)*

The Campaign against the Acts was based on the violation of women's civil rights, the unequal treatment of men and women under the Acts and on the implication that the government condoned immorality and the use of prostitutes by the armed forces.

The Acts were finally repealed in 1883 after a campaign lasting for fourteen years, that involved mass meetings during parliamentary elections and by-elections. The campaign was aimed particularly at the new male working-class voters because it was working-class women who suffered under the Acts. Working-class women who were designated prostitutes were encouraged in resistance to the Acts by the payment of their legal expenses if they fought through the courts. There was also resistance in working-class neighbourhoods which was either spontaneous or organised by local women. This co-existed with conventional philanthropic 'rescue' work. In Bristol the campaigners ran the Old Park Hospital as a voluntary treatment centre in opposition to compulsory treatment and registration under the Acts. [29]

After 1884 hopes of a rapid achievement of the vote for women became harder to sustain, and divisions which had previously been containable became increasingly serious. [30]

One of these divisions was over the position of married women, after the Married Women's Property Act of 1882 extended control over property and earnings to married women who were not separated or divorced or widowed. Previously, the argument for the vote had tended to stress the right to a vote of 'self-supporting women of the trading and working classes, the widows and the spinster' (Mrs Beddoe). While men's right to vote remained based on property qualification, and women's right to own property or to retain earnings after marriage was extremely limited, this did not constitute a practical problem for the movement.

Afterwards, a very complicated set of issues opened up. Should the vote be extended only to self-supporting unmarried women, widows and those separated from their husbands, who had no husband to 'represent their interests'; should it be extended to married women who were ratepayers in their own right (i.e. those wealthy enough to own property themselves in the form of a house or a business); or should married women be recognised as joint householders or occupiers as could happen with two men living together? Jessie Craigen, a supporter of the rights of married women to vote, was one of the visiting speakers in the West of England during the 1880s. She wrote that the passing of the Act highlighted contradictory beliefs in the movement. Some members and supporters argued that married women should be excluded, 'not because they have no property, not because they are women, but because they are married'. She said that many others could not accept this: 'It is the representation of womanhood they desire, and not the representation merely of rate book, or an acre of mud, or a pile of bricks and mortar'. (31)

The conflict was partly between the more radical belief that the vote should be the right of each individual citizen and the more conservative idea that it represented an 'interest' or a household and that a man could adequately represent the 'interest' of his wife. But there were other complications as well.

Women were in a majority and it was believed that it would be unthinkable that a majority of women electors would be acceptable to Parliament or the country. A succession of Liberal Governments hamstrung bill after bill because they would neither accept a democratic measure that would lead to a potential majority of women electors or a restricted franchise for women which would probably favour the conservatives.

Women's party affiliations became increasingly important, leading to a split in the movement nationally in 1888 over the admission of organisations which had aims other than women's suffrage. In practice this would have largely meant Liberal Women's organisations, some of which, like that in Bristol, were deeply committed to votes for women. Others were more purely party-oriented and formed largely to replace the work done by paid male canvassers after the Corrupt Practices Act of 1883 had made such payment illegal. (32) The two parts of the movement did not reunite until 1898. Throughout the split, however, the two factions co-operated wherever possible and refused to attack one another. (33)

Women active in the Bristol movement have left no record of their feelings on these issues. The report of 1890 speaks of the need to 'press forward the special work of this society which lies outside mere "party" interests' and trusting that 'women of all classes and political parties will aid them in carrying it on to a successful issue'. It seems from the Report of 1889-90 that more and more activities by politically interested women were going into party activity. The suffrage society comforted itself that 'active work by women of all parties, the Conservative Primrose League, the Women's Liberal Association, wives of candidates "at the front" speaking for their husbands' meant that 'the old asseveration that women have nothing to do with politics has had its complete

BRISTOL AND WEST OF ENGLAND BRANCH

OF THE

NATIONAL SOCIETY FOR WOMEN'S SUFFRAGE.

Office: 69 PARK STREET, BRISTOL.

Treasurer: MRS. ASHWORTH HALLETT.

Hon. Secs. { MRS. ASHWORTH HALLETT.
MISS EVA TRIBE.

The Committee earnestly beg friends who are interested in the object of the Society to aid their work by contributing to its Funds.

Form to be filled in by Person desirous of Promoting the Object of the Society.

Madam,

I authorise you to add my name to the List of Members of the National Society for Women's Suffrage, and I enclose a Subscription of £ _____

Donation of £ _____ to the funds of the Bristol and West of England Branch.

Signed _____

Name and Address { _____
for post. { _____

To MISS EVA TRIBE, *Hon. Sec.,* 7 Westfield Park, Bristol.

quietus'.

The Bristol and West of England Society continued to publish pamphlets, arguments, and appeals, in favour of parliamentary suffrage and explaining the operation of the municipal and county vote to women ratepayers. But Miss Tanner, the secretary during part of the period, contrasts 'the interval between the two great Reform Bills when hopes were high' with the period between 1884 and 1904 when suffrage supporters were 'disheartened but kept working'. (The period between 1904 and 1918 saw what she described as a resurgence of the movement, with new young members and 'fresh active propaganda'.) (34)

The mid-1880s had brought the women's suffrage movement up against apparently immoveable obstacles, and this must have been all the more frustrating because it was obvious, as the Bristol Report of 1889-90 had said, that considerable numbers of women had emerged from mid-Victorian purdah. Even those who were opponents of the suffrage had to leave the seclusion of the family hearthside and thrust themselves into the public eye to make their revulsion against women's demand for political rights known. Whereas in the 1850s a few individual women had tentatively taken up important causes, by the 1880s there were a large number of women's organisations - including organisations of working-class women. Women were municipal and county electors and had become members of local school boards, boards of guardians, and other similar bodies. The women's rights movement had a series of victories behind it including the repeal of the Contagious Diseases Acts, Divorce Legislation, Legal Separation in cases of Aggravated Assault and the Married Women's Property Acts.

Many women in the suffrage movement, and not women alone, had from the beginning been concerned with more than the vote for its own sake. Many women who were reformers like Mary Carpenter in Bristol, Florence Nightingale, and Josephine Butler, the leader of the campaign against the Contagious Diseases Act, were, or became, suffrage supporters, even if it was sometimes felt better to separate the issues for practical or tactical reasons. This was as true in Bristol as anywhere else.

Elizabeth Sturge, in her memoirs (35) records the active interest of the women of her family - her mother, her sisters, especially the elder, Emily, and her cousin from Birmingham - in many aspects of women's rights apart from the vote. They, and other members of the suffrage movement in Bristol, were involved in the movement against the Contagious Diseases Act which was launched in Bristol at the Victoria Rooms and had many strong supporters in the city.

Suffragists like the Sturges were interested in education, both of the working class and of women and girls. The Sturges attended the Lectures for Ladies (the forerunner of Bristol University College). They helped to found Redland High School for Girls in 1882. (Clifton High School for Girls had been founded through the efforts of Catherine Winkworth, another Bristol suffragist in 1887.)

Elizabeth Sturge herself was also interested in the provision of decent housing for working-class people. After having worked with Octavia Hill (36) in London she helped towards the establishment of Shirehampton as a Garden Suburb. (There had been an earlier attempt at a working-class housing project in the Jacobs Wells area, near the present St Peter's House flats, in 1875. This was started by Susannah Winkworth, another suffragist, who has had Winkworth Place, St Pauls, named after her.)

As the achievement of the vote seemed blocked, more and more women became involved in a whole variety of movements and organisations. In the early period, especially, the differences between philanthropic and radical activities were not always clear. Many women and men who became prominent in radical and socialist activity did so initially through religious or philanthropic impulses.

Working-class women did become involved in the suffrage movement (as Jill Liddington and Jill Norris have shown for Manchester). They were involved in the campaign against the Contagious Diseases Act and there was also some union organisation among women from the mid-seventies on, though it was difficult and spasmodic. From the mid-eighties working-class married women began to be involved in political activity through the Co-operative Women's Guilds, which took an active interest in gaining the vote for women, particularly married working-class women.

The first Co-operative Women's Guild was formed in Bristol in the winter of 1889-90. The oldest guild still functioning was founded in Bedminster in November 1892. The Bedminster Guild's minutes and programme (37) record the connections it had with suffragists through invited speakers. These included both Miss Tanner and Mary Clifford. (Topics included Women in Local Government, Report from the Leeds Women Workers Conference, Children under the Poor Law, The Aliens Bill, War or Peace. There was also a concern with co-operative principles and practice, labour conditions and general self education (38).) As early as 16 October 1893 the Bedminster Guild passed a unanimous resolution in favour of women's suffrage after a talk by Mrs Martin, Secretary of the Women's Liberal Association. It is likely that significant numbers of Bristol suffragists, both men and women, were radical liberals, like many of the sponsors and committee members whose names are recorded, just as most early trade unionists and co-operators were.

Mrs Beddoe believed that the early campaigners for women's rights 'certainly became socialists in the best sense of the word'. She was sympathetic to the granting of the vote to farm labourers in 1884 - 'It was decided that the farm labourer must have the vote to protect his interests - and quite right too' - but commented that, 'It is almost laughable that women are the only people whose interests are supposed not to need the guardianship which political power now confers'. (39)

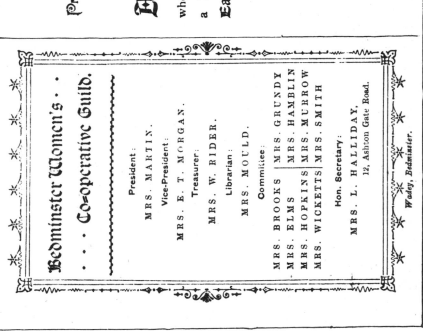

Preliminary * Announcement.

A Public Meeting will be held the last week in October, when Mr. O'Callagban will give a Lecture on "Fruits of the Earth," with lantern illustrations.

Further particulars later on.

Bedminster Women's Co-operative Guild.

President:
MRS. MARTIN.

Vice-President:
MRS. E. T. MORGAN.

Treasurer:
MRS. W. RIDER.

Librarian:
MRS. MOULD.

Committee:

MRS. BROOKS	MRS. GRUNDY
MRS. ELMS	MRS. HAMBLIN
MRS. HOPKINS	MRS. MURROW
MRS. WICKETTS	MRS. SMITH

Hon. Secretary:
MRS. L. HALLIDAY,
12, Ashton Gate Road.

Wadey, Bedminster.

Front page of Bedminster Women's Co-operative Guild programme for 1896-7

Bedminster Women's Co-operative Guild programme 1896-7

* * Programme. * *

Winter Session, 1896-7,

EAST STREET STORES, 3 P.M.

Oct. 12	"Dividend"	Mrs. L. HALLIDAY
„ 26	"My work as a Guardian"	Miss E. F. EVANS
Nov. 9	"Co-operation"	Mrs. MOULD
„ 23	"War or Peace"	Miss TANNER
Dec. 7	Half-yearly Meeting	
„ 21	No Meeting	
1897.		
Jan. 4	Social	Mrs. MORGAN
„ 18	"History of the Poor Law"	Mrs. W. RIDER
Feb. 1	"How our movement grew"	Miss MAY
„ 15	Paper by Mrs. PHILLIPS (Secretary Totterdown Branch).	
Mar. 1	"Temperance"	Mrs. J. J. MARTIN
„ 15	"Laundries and Laundry Work"	
„ 29	"Bristol Riots"	Mrs. MARTIN
Apr 12	Social	Mrs. GOUGH
„ 26	"Condition of Employment of Women and Girls in Co-operative Stores"	Mrs. GRUNDY
May 10	Half-yearly Meeting.	

A Dressmaking Class will be held at the Stores every Alternate Monday from 3 to 4.30 p.m.

East St Stores
Guild Meeting held — Oct 16th 93

Vice President Mrs Dalby in the chair
Present The Treasurer & Assistant Secretary
Committee members present Messrs Andrew,
Robson, Brooks, C Halliday & W Donnett,
There were 30 members present
The minutes of the previous meeting were
read and confirmed
Mrs Martin Secretary of the Womens Liberal
Association then gave an address on Womens
Suffrage which was listened to with marked
attention, A resolution was passed in favour
of Womens Suffrage, and carried unanimously
A vote of thanks (was proposed by Mrs Gough
seconded by Mrs Cooksley) to Mrs Martin
for her kindness in giving such an
interesting address.
The sum of 10s 9 7 Pence was collected
towards the purchase of a piano at the
close of the meeting making a total of
four shillings and 7 pence
F Morgan Confirmed

A page taken from the Minute book of the Bedminster Women's Co-op Guild 1893.

Anne Priestman, who was later to support strike action by the Barton Hill cotton mill women and others, had called for the unionisation of women at the Victoria Rooms, Bristol, in 1875 (in a paper to the Economic Section of the British Association Meeting in Bristol on 30 August 1875). In her paper 'The Industrial Position of Women as Affected by their Exclusion from the Suffrage' (40) she argued that women needed union organisation and the vote as well, to ensure that laws like the Factory Act of 1874, apparently passed for their protection, really represented their interests rather than leading to an arbitrary exclusion from better-paid work and from training in skilled trades. She said that many trade unions 'forbid their members to take a girl as an apprentice' and that, 'In some cases the laws of the country hamper and harrass women while they leave men free, so that little by little women sink down so low that here, in the City of Bristol, there are women keeping themselves alive without complaint, but without hope, on making shirts for 2¼d each'. Her belief that the interests of working women were not represented by 'the class of men to whom they belong' must have been confirmed by the rejection by the newly-formed Trades Council in 1874 of an appeal to help in organising a union among the women workers at the Great Western Cotton Mill at Barton Hill, and by its later exclusion of women from its Labour League of 1885. (41)

A body called the National Union of Working Women was formed in Bristol in 1874 as a result of discussions around Anne Priestman's paper and with the participation of Emma Patterson, a pioneer of women's unions. The NUWW was represented at the TUC for a number of years. (42) The problem of whether to rely on legislation or collective bargaining to improve the conditions of working people was a cause of dispute in the TUC at the time, especially in relation to women who were less organised than men industrially and lacked any electoral power. Marion Ramelson in *Petticoat Rebellion* quotes part of the debate, which was given a sharp edge because some of the men like Henry Broadhurst, a stonemason who was later to become an anti-women's suffrage Liberal MP, had in mind the idea of 'protecting' women out of the labour market altogether. Some of the women's advocates, like Emma Patterson, took a 'classic' liberal position on legislation, believing that protective legislation would put women at a disadvantage in the labour market and preferring to work for unionisation to put them in a stronger bargaining position. We do not know in detail about the relationship between Bristol suffragists and the NUWW after its founding, but it is clear that Bristol suffragists like the Priestmans and Mrs Beddoe, although themselves middle-class, were concerned with the problems of working-class women as well as wanting to widen employment opportunities for women of all classes. There would be no clear distinction between Liberal and Labour interests for years to come.

In the next twenty years the differences would become clearer. The critical distinction, among suffrage supporters, as among other reformers, was to be whether they wished to help in generating action among working women themselves for economic and social change, or whether they believed in legislative or charitable action to ease distress, without challenging the economic and social structure or the power of the employing class. These differences were apparent in the cotton workers strike of 1889. One of the Priestman sisters set up a soup kitchen in support of the strike,(43) giving the strike committee itself fifty tickets a day to distribute, while Mary Clifford, a moderate suffragist and leader of the NUWW, (44) despite her genuine sympathy for the poor, saw them as always in need of guidance from above, in both a social and religious sense. In a letter to a friend, as the strike ended on 28 November, 1889, she wrote:

> *The cotton people went to work this morning. No increase in wages, but many grievances redressed. We are having a heavy time tackling these huge labour questions and have been meeting some of the men and women privately. The women are at present very open to being led, the men very full of reasoning of the socialist kind... I think there is much more to come on all hands. They have offered to take us into their counsels. Personally I don't think I can do it...But my mind goes out to these women and girls. I am going over to see some of them on Saturday. One can only pray - the first four petitions of the Lord's prayer.(45)*

Anne and Mary Priestman seem to have left no memoirs, though their letters to Josephine Butler are in The Fawcett Library. They survived into the twentieth century to support Annie Kenney when she came to Bristol to set up a branch of the Women's Social and Political Union in 1908 (as did Lilias Ashworth Hallett and Maria Colby), and continued to give support to the WSPU through the period of militancy. (46) This was another divide on which they were on the opposite side from Mary Clifford, who shrank from militancy in any cause.

Early attempts to organise women into unions seem to have been shortlived, but there was renewed activity from 1889 onwards, particularly, among unskilled workers. In Bristol women workers from the cotton factory and the tobacco industry were prominent in the strikes of 1889. In 1892 the striking Sander's confectionery women of Redcliffe joined the striking dockers in the demonstration in the Horsefair which led to the charge by Dragoons and Hussars that became known as Black Friday. In both these strikes middle-class women who were socialists and suffragists played a leading part .

In 1889, 'Bristol City became a seething centre of revolt' in the movement to organise unskilled and semi-skilled workers into trade unions:

> *Without organisation, funds, or preparation of any kind, various bodies of workers struck for higher wages and better conditions of work. The operatives engaged at the Barton Hill works 'came out' for an all-round*

revision of the terms of their employment (October, 1889). Headed by
Miriam Daniell and Jas. Vickery, the women and girls paraded day
after day from the factory gates through the city to Clifton, and in the
evening of October 25th, 1889, they had a meeting of 4,000 people at
the Ropewalk. (S. Bryher, Pt, II p. 16.)

After the demonstration a meeting of sympathisers was held and a Bristol
strike committee set up to 'render every possible assistance to the, at present,
unorganised workers of Bristol...of both sexes'. When the cotton workers
appealed for help and showed themselves to be determined not to go back to
work, despite their lack of a union and lack of funds, the committee, especially
Miriam Daniell, Helena Born, Robert Weare, Irving, Gore and Watson, [47]
organised public campaigns to attract funds, including 'more processions
through the city' and to churches:

Sunday mornings the strikers with clean white aprons and shawls over
their heads paraded to various places of worship, such as Christchurch,
St Paul's Clifton, Highbury Chapel, etc., and this all helped to focus
public attention. (Bryher, Pt 11, p. 18.)

Miriam Daniell and Helena Born were among those putting forward the
'reasoning of the socialist kind' deplored by Mary Clifford. They were also
involved in attempts to unionise 'the ill-paid seamstresses who worked in their
homes scattered over the country around Bristol'. A union was formed, but the
isolation of the homeworkers from one another made progress difficult
(Bryher, Pt 11, p7). As members of the Bristol Socialist Society, Miriam and
Helena were prominent in its educational work, speaking on such subjects as
'Why Women Should Organise', 'The Aristocracy of Sex', and the 'Evolution
of Women'. Miriam, an artist, designed and made a banner for the Society
depicting the flaming heart of freedom. They were 'ethical socialists' and
friends of the socialist writer, Edward Carpenter, like other members of the
Socialist Society, including Robert Gilliard, the Sharland brothers and later
Katharine Conway and Enid Stacey. Helena and Miriam had left Clifton to live
in St Philips among working-class people. They have left no record of their
day-to-day political activities in Bristol, though we do have some knowledge of
their ideas and style of life. [48] Miriam had left her husband to live with Helena.
Comment surrounding their open Lesbian relationship contributed in their
decision to leave Bristol for a utopian socialist community in America. [49]
Helena had worked with the Women's Liberal Association. She explained her
changed political ideas to a friend in the Association like this:

Equality and freedom for women is one phase of an ideal of universal
freedom and equality. I have not taken up a new position without

Lilias Ashworth (Mrs Hallett),

Mrs Beddoe,

Millicent Garrett (Mrs Henry Fawcett).

Drawings by Sarah Braun

thinking it out... The principles of Socialism as I understand them, seem to me economically incontrovertible, and to comprise spiritual ideals of unity and brotherhood which alone can transmute the materialism of our time. And I feel that the only way to convince others of the truth of one's principles, and to bring about the new time, is by living them...
It is uphill work, but we cannot isolate ourselves from the mass... To the loyal there is a joy, as Whitman says, in 'being tossed in the brave turmoil of these times'. (Bryher, Pt 11, p6-7.)

The Bristol Socialists believed in making the connections between their politics and everyday lives. They organised teas, dances and theatrical events from 1887 onwards to widen their appeal beyond the small group of activists, mainly men, who were the original society members. Socialism involved, for Helena Born and her comrades, democracy in sexual relationships and a change in the personal attitudes of both men and women, (50) not just the formal entry of women into political life and trade union activity. Believers in simplicity of life combined with beauty, Helena and Miriam were unconventional in dress, tastes, and habits, but they were also hard working, tireless organisers, working with exploited women workers. In the cotton strike they gathered 'through their incessant efforts' funds 'from all parts of the country':

Night upon night, after days of unremitting activity, into the small hours they sat counting the pennies taken up at local meetings and strike parades and planning the judicious disbursement of the money among the needy strikers. (Tufts, quoted in Rowbotham, and Weekes p71.)

To organise the seamstresses Helena might tramp thirty miles in a day, but was not able to build a lasting and vigorous union. Helena believed in the need for men and women workers to organise together in an equal partnership. She approved of the Gas Workers and General Labourers Union of which Eleanor Marx was one of the founders, and which the striking cotton workers joined, because it was 'one of the few unions initiated by men which accords women full representation on its councils, and has included among its objects obtaining, wherever possible, the same wages for women doing the same work as men'. (Tufts, Rowbotham, p70.)

The Gas Workers Union was also chosen by the Sander's Confectionery Workers in their attempts to organise in the autumn of 1892. The 'sweet girls' were central to the wave of strikes and demonstrations in that year as the cotton workers had been in 1889. Like the cotton workers they paraded on Sundays to the churches in Clifton and Cotham, particularly Highbury Chapel at the top of St Michaels Hill where their employer was a member of the congregation.

Enid Stacy was Secretary of the Sander's workers strike committee in 1892. She had become Secretary of the Association for the Promotion of Trade

Unionism Amongst Women when Miriam Daniell left for the United States with Helena Born in 1890.(51)

Enid was already a socialist by 1889. Once she had finished her studies she became caught up in activity in support of the striking cotton workers. She described one of the strike processions to her own parish church at All Saints, Clifton, 'wet and desperate after many weeks of sullen holding out for even a right to combine':

> *Soon she was literally tramping the soles off her boots busily engaged making collections and organising work of every description...(Bryher, Pt 11, p22.)*

For Katherine St John Conway, the sight of 'sister-women'...ill-clad, wet through with the driving rain, hungry...'out on strike against starvation wages and for the right to combine' (Bryher, p29-31) was a decisive moment in her life. She too joined the 1889 strike committee and later, after her marriage to Bruce Glazier, became a leading figure in the ILP and the Women's Labour League.

Enid's artist father's studio was already a socialist meeting place, described by Katherine Conway in later years as 'some enchanted Hall of Dreams':

> *There was music and song and dance. Enid's sisters were wonderful dancers... Night after night bands of socialists young and old, would meet for study and debate, and terribly practical work, too, for the unemployed and unskilled workers... Never did our meetings break up without our singing one of Morris' songs to a crooning Irish melody...(Bryher ibid.)*

Enid, who had won the first Catherine Winkworth scholarship for girls to Bristol University College, took a London B.A. in 1890 but had to leave Bristol to earn a living after being deprived of coaching work by Redland High School, where she had also been a pupil, because of her socialist activities, (52) particularly during the 1892 strikes. The history of Redland High School only states that she 'devoted her life to social work...child welfare and the improvement of conditions for women workers'. (53) In fact, Edith became a tireless and gifted speaker and writer for the causes of women and socialism, and a member of the ILP executive before her death in 1903 aged 35. She believed in women organising for themselves as well as for socialism. In 1891 she successfully resisted a proposal to merge the Association for the Promotion of Trade Unionism amongst women with the Bristol Socialist Society Organising Committee.

The 'sweet girls' strike began over the dismissal of workers who had joined the Gas Workers Union. The 300 workers 'had many grievances, hours were long; excessive fines were imposed; during their dinner hour the women were actually locked in; only two or three being allowed out to fetch meals for the rest; average pay for a fifty-hour week was 4s.7¾d. Breaking point came when a fifteen-minute rest time was withdrawn and hours were extended by an hour to 7p.m.' A work stoppage and approach to Enid's committee and the Gas Workers Union brought a suspension of the extension of hours, but dismissals began when women began to join the union. (54)

The women, nicknamed 'Sander's White Slaves', were later joined on their parades by the Trades Council (who 'established a precedent by participating in a Sunday parade for the first time in their history') (55) and after that by striking deal runners from the port, and locked-out dockers. The confectionery workers, deal runners and dockers arranged a joint lantern parade from the Grove to the Horsefair for Friday, 23 December to raise funds for the strikers' families at Christmas. This 'resulted in one of the worst instances of local official blundering and terrorism within living memory'. (56)

After a police objection to 'torches' being carried, a deputation met the chief constable who appeared satisfied of their peaceful intentions.

By the day of the march a squadron each of the Dragoons and Hussars had been brought in to reinforce the police, the carrying of Chinese lanterns had been forbidden, and the marches instructed to keep to a route prescribed by the police which bypassed the city centre. Since the deal runners announced that they would accept the ban on lanterns but not the prescribed route, the women's strike committee decided to withdraw the women from the procession because of the danger of violent police action if the strikers insisted on their freedom to choose their own route. On the night of 23 December the march followed three separate routes from The Grove to the Horsefair. (57)

One section of the demonstration was batoned by police when it tried to go through to Wine Street or High Street from Bridge Street. Later, at the Horsefair meeting, where the confectionery workers and the dock workers had separate platforms, the concentration of police 'excited hostile feeling amongst some portion of the crowd' which was increased 'when a body of the Dragoons passed through Lower Union Street to the police station'... After that, 'matters became quieter until... Charles Jarman was arrested for alleged incitement to riot... Then, in the subsequent disturbance the police charged the more aggressive of the crowd'. The Dragoons were called out just before 9.30 and 'pursued the crowd round the Horsefair and through the streets in the vicinity'. There were large numbers of reported injuries and several arrests, including that of Ben Tillett for 'incitement to riot' in a speech on the previous Sunday. The weekend before his trial was marked by enormous meetings in The Grove, off Queen Square, an estimated seven to eight thousand on the Saturday:

Next morning (Sunday) Sander's girls and the dockers joined forces in another procession. In spite of the drizzling rain, five or six thousand joined the ranks and paraded through the city to the Grove where two monster meetings were held. Tillett again spoke, and was supported by Dr Aveling, in addition to local speakers. (Bryher, Pt 11, p47. A description of Black Friday and its aftermath is contained on pp. 38-49.)

The events of Black Friday gained national publicity because of the trial and acquittal of Ben Tillet in London, though Charles Jarman and two others had been quietly convicted of incitement to riot before a Bristol court and sentenced to three months in prison. The sweet workers' strike was ended after twenty-six weeks with some wage gains but no union recognition. The deal runners were later to go back to work 'on terms far short of what they had hoped for'.

The strike committee admitted defeat on the union issue and found the Sander's strikers other better-paid work, but they did not regard the strike campaign as totally defeated:

The vigorous way in which the strike was carried on was the primary means of arousing the great attention in this part of the country to the Labour Question now so prominent; not the least successful result of which is the great increase in membership to the Trade Unions. Moreover, it was the means of raising the standard of wages, with improved conditions to the workers engaged in both this and other factories. (Bryher, Pt 11, p.490.)

Another result was the subsequent election of the first Labour representatives to the Bedminster Board of Guardians.

By the time the strikes had ended Enid Stacy had left Bristol to work in the North of England. Here, unlike Katharine St John Conway, who also became a nationally important ILP worker, she became involved in the beginnings of a new wave of Women's Suffrage activity. She was a member of the Manchester National Society for Women's Suffrage and spoke there at the first annual meeting of the National Union of Women's Suffrage Societies, the newly united organisation following the split of 1888. She became a friend of Esther Roper, whom she accompanied on a suffrage deputation of women graduates to Westminster in 1903, shortly before her death. By 1894 the ILP Conference had voted in favour of extending the suffrage to women as well as men, but Enid Stacy believed that there was a gap between theory and practice in the party. She carried on a debate about Labour movement attitudes to women in the socialist paper the *Clarion* in 1894 and 1896, and ran an article in the form of a dialogue between two male socialists in the *Labour Prophet*, the Labour Churches monthly paper in 1894:

B. *Since I've joined this movement I've not cared much for home. Wife scolds at me so, and goes on about me being away so much, not caring for her, neglecting the children... Why, the very name 'Labour Movement' or 'Socialism' is enough to send her into a regular tantrum. You would think me one of the worst men going, and yet I never fail to give her nearly all my wage on Fridays, and she certainly cannot say that she ever saw me drunk in all her life. What more she can expect I don't know!*

A. *Well, it strikes me, she may perhaps expect such things as affection and your companionship - you don't mind me speaking straight?*

B. *No, of course not...only how can you talk of companionship? Why, what have we got in common? You can't expect women to take any interest, as a whole, on those matters. They aren't capable of it. They are too conventional and afraid of the parson, and...*

A. *Stop, stop. Don't go on so fast...perhaps it doesn't strike you there are are two sides...*(58)

In her work for both the ILP and the movement for women's suffrage, Enid Stacy 'developed some of the vital theoretical framework to bring socialist and feminist ideas together for the first time', but never losing the 'ability to identify with those women who were expected to get on with their housework and take no part in political experiences' with their husbands, as well as with the underpaid women in the labour force. (59)

She wrote an important essay, 'A Century of Women's Rights', which was printed in Edward Carpenter's *Forecasts of the Coming Century*, in 1897, in which she described the achievements of the early women's rights movement while criticising the limitations of the 'gospel of individual rights' on which it was largely based. Going on to list what remained to be achieved:

The right to choose whether or not to have children;
equality within marriage and fairer divorce laws;
the right of mothers to guardianship of their children;
full legal and political rights, including the vote in both local and parliamentary elections;
and freedom as workers so that as much protective legislation as possible applied to men as well as women workers. Only then would men and women achieve the socialist goal of a true co-operative commonwealth. (Liddington & Norris, p131.)

Enid Stacy died at the age of 35 in 1903, having 'undermined her originally fine physique by unresting labours, constant open-air speaking, constant journeying, poor food, uncomfortable quarters' (Syliva Pankhurst). But it has been said that:

> *'A Century of Women's Rights'* remained the most comprehensive statement of women's claims within the ILP and labour movement for many years. Like Ester Roper in the North of England Society, Enid Stacy as a middle-class woman had a vital role to play during a period when working-class women's organisations were only just beginning to provide their own experienced and capable leaders. (*Liddington & Norris, p.131.*)

In Bristol no-one seems to have replaced her or Katharine Conway for some time. Unspectacular work went on after 1890. Co-operative Women's Guilds were formed in various parts of Bristol and Mrs Tillett, Mrs Lloyd and Mrs Webb were among the early Labour Guardians of the poor. At some time before the First World War, an ILP women's organisation was formed. (60) The Bristol and West of England Suffrage Society had continued working as best it could but it would not, in Miss Tanner's words, be 'coming out into the open again' until after 1904. It was then overtaken by a new wave of militant suffrage activity.

From 1908 onwards Bristol became the centre of Annie Kenney's highly successful attempts to build the Women's Social and Political Union (Suffragettes) in the West of England. The activity was spread throughout Bristol, particularly during a general election period when three or more meetings a day in different parts of Bristol were not unusual. From here the organisation was spread as far as Devon and Cornwall, being particularly vigorous and continuous in Bath and Bristol. As well as organising meetings, leafleting, and selling the Suffragette weekly paper *'Votes for Women'* the WSPU in Bristol organised a spectacular theatrical event, a Pageant, play and concert with a cast of hundreds in the Princess Theatre in 1910. (61) They also arranged a mass refusal to register in the census of 1911 by women who believed they should not be counted as citizens if they did not have the right to vote.

In the period of militancy, when they campaigned against Liberal Cabinet ministers and heckled them at meetings, Theresa Garnett was arrested and imprisoned in Horfield goal for an attack on Winston Churchill at Temple Meads Station, in November 1909. (62)

Suffragettes twice hid overnight in the Colston Hall organ to avoid being excluded from Cabinet ministers' meetings where by this time women were sometimes admitted only if accompanied by men known to the organisers.

In the period of attacks on property in 1913/14, they burned a timber yard, a mansion at Frenchay and another at Stoke Bishop, and the University Sports Pavilion at Coombe Dingle. (63) After this last event, their shop and headquarters in Queens Road, opposite the University, were gutted by fire and

"BRISTOL 'VARSITY STUDENTS REVENGE." THE WRECKED SUFFRAGETTES HEADQUARTERS.

In 1913 some Bristol University students wrecked the headquarters of the Bristol Suffragette movement in Park Street.

looted by students. (64) Their more day-to-day activity included massive door-to-door canvassing of women who had been given the municipal vote, meetings for working women in Bedminster and other areas, jumble sales, lectures, and so on. Horfield gaol was used for the detention of numbers of suffragette prisoners, some of whom carried out hunger strikes there.

Through all this, the non-militant Bristol and West of England Women's Suffrage Society continued to exist and carry out their own activities, organising marches and electoral work. They joined with the militants in many of the campaigns except those involving attacks on property, and expressed their support of hunger strikers, particularly by opposing the Governments' 'Cat and Mouse Act'. (This allowed the release of suffragettes weakened by hunger strikes and forced feeding and their re-arrest when recovered, until they had served out their sentences in full.)

The difference between the WSPU and other suffragists were not only about campaigning methods. Other militant groups, like the Women's Freedom League, had left because of its undemocratic structure. (The WSPU came to rest on the idea of unquestioning obedience to Emmeline Pankhurst and her eldest daughter Christabel.) The Pethick-Lawrences, who had financed the WSPU and ran its paper up to 1912, and Sylvia Pankhurst, were edged out, while Annie Kenney, despite conflicts of loyalties that were sometimes agonising, continued to accept Christabel's 'Generalship'. (65) Throughout all these conflicts, public argument was avoided as far as possible.

Other groups of women, especially those from the Labour and Cooperative movements could not accept that women's suffrage must take first place before any other reforms, nor that any who disagreed should be treated as opponents. At this time there were many disagreements on tactics and principle behind the various Women's Suffrage Bills coming before the House of Commons. To previous disagreements over married women and property qualifications were added the question of Adult Suffrage. Women suffragists rightly suspected that many Adult suffragists would drop their insistence on equality between the sexes given the possibility of manhood suffrage. This is what they did do in 1918 when all men over 21 were given the vote while suffrage for women was limited to those over 30. Similarly, opponents of granting suffrage based on property qualifications were prepared to accept property qualifications for women voters only in the 1918 Act.

During the war period in Bristol, as elsewhere, possibilities of paid work for women expanded enormously. Work hours often meant that women would be out in the streets long after dark. In this period a new women's organisation was formed in Bristol, the Women Patrols and Police, and a training school was set up with the aim of gaining official recognition. The Patrols were formed for the protection of women on the streets from physical attack and 'moral danger'.

The movement seems to have been a rather strange mixture of middle-class social work, police work, and the defence of women. It involved women like Mary Allen, who had been a hunger-striker, as well as 'moderates'. (66) After the women's police patrols came under the control of the Home Office, an organisation called Bristol Women's Aid was formed which combined the protection of women against street assault and helping women in the courts, particularly unmarried mothers who were trying to obtain affiliation orders so that they would not be faced with the work-house or separation from their children.(67)

As with the nineteenth century, there are still huge gaps in what we know of women's movements in Bristol in the early twentieth century. What we do know contradicts the simple picture of a middle-class movement for women's rights quite separate from working-class women's movements and the Labour and socialist movements.

Throughout the whole period up to and after the First World War, lines of class and ideology on women's issues were often fluid and confused. While women's organisations often supported each other across class and party lines, there were divisions of interest within classes and political parties along sex lines, just as there had been in the nineteenth century.

(1)   The Radical Reform Associations of 1819 were part of a movement for electoral reform concentrated in Yorkshire and Lancashire. Their demands included "Annual Parliaments and Universal Suffrage". Some were female associations. Their march to St Peter's Field Manchester on Monday 16th August 1819 was led by "a hundred or so women". The demonstration, which became known by the name "Peterloo" was attacked by the military with many resulting injuries and some loss of life. It was followed by arrests and trials, some for High Treason. (See for example: Marion Ramelson, *The Petticoat Rebellion*, Lawrence and Wishart, 1967, Ch. 6, Dorothy Thompson, *"Women and Nineteenth Century Radical Politics"*, in Juliet Mitchell and Ann Oakley (eds), *The Rights and Wrongs of Women*, Penguin, 1976).

(2)   The Chartist Movement for electoral reform drew up a six point charter which included annual elections for parliament, equal electoral districts, payment for members of parliament, universal (or manhood) suffrage, secret ballots and the abolition of property qualifications for members of parliament. (D. Thompson, op.cit)

(3)   Dorothy Thompson. op cit., p. 120, 124, 127

(4)   See for example: Sheila Rowbotham, *Hidden from History*, Pluto Press, 1973.
        Jo O'Brien, *Women's Liberation in Labour History*, Spokesman Pamphlet, No 24 Nottingham, no date.

(5)   Harold Goldman, *Emma Patterson*, Lawrence and Wishart, 1974. Dorothy Thompson, op. cit., p. 113-5.

(6)   Jill Liddington and Jill Norris, *One Hand tied Behind Us*, Virago 1978 Hannah Mitchell, *The Hard Way Up*, Sylvia Pankhurst, *The Suffragettes Movement*, Virago, 1977.

(7)   So far this is not generally well known though they are mentioned in several general studies of the nineteenth century women's movement, such as: Roger Fulton, *Votes for Women*, Faber (1957), Antonia Raeburn, *Militant suffragettes*, New English Library, (1973), and in Marion Ramelson, op.cit. There is also contemporary material in the memoirs and biographies of prominent workers for women's rights and women's suffrage, a number of whom lived and worked in the area or had close personal contacts here; see for example: Helen Blackburn, *A History of Women's Suffrage*, (1902) in Fawcett Library, London, Bertha Mason, *The Story of the Women's Suffrage Movement*, in University of Bristol School of Education Library and memoirs by Mill Millicent Fawcett, Annie Kenney, Emmeline Pethick-Lawrence. Local sources include: A.M. Beddoe, *The Early Years of the Women's Suffrage Movement* Bradford on Avon (1911), S. J. Tanner *How the Women's Suffrage Movement was founded in Bristol fifty years ago*. Bristol (1918), both in Avon County Reference Library and a recent pamphlet based on the diaries of the Blathwayt family of

Batheaston, E. Wilmott Dobbie, *A Nest of Suffragettes in Somerset*, Batheaston Society, 290 High St, Batheaston, Bath BA1 7RA. (Mary Blathwayt was a WSPU organiser in Bath and Bristol).

(8)   John Cannon, *The Chartists in Bristol*, Bristol Branch of the Historical Association, (1964) p.9.

(9)   op cit

(10)   Dorothy Thompson op cit., p.131.
Marion Ramelson op cit., p.70.

(11)   Dorothy Thompson, op.cit., p.137-8.

(12)   See The Estlin Papers, Microfilm in Avon County Reference Library of the collection in Dr Williams Library, London. The Radical Abolitionists campaigned to make slavery illegal throughout the United States, including the Southern States, where it was already the basis of the economy and its extension into the new southern territories as well as north of the Mason-Dixon line.
The less radical tended to concentrate on preventing the extension of slavery especially to the new northern areas of settlement. The Radicals helped slaves to escape to Canada by way of an "underground railway" of sympathisers. This was regarded as an attack on property rights in Britain as well as in the USA and was one of the factors in the rising tensions which led to the American Civil War. For connections between the Anti - Slavery Movement and the American and British Women's Rights Movements see Marion Ramelson op cit p. 73-4.

(13)   Estlin Papers, Reel 3.

(14)   Estlin Papers, Reel 3.

(15)   Estlin Papers: Reel 3
English Woman's Review, Vol 14, June 15th (1803).

(16)   Helen Blackburn *A History of Women's Suffrage*, (1902), Fawcett Library p.60.

(17)   Mr Commissioner Hill afterwards Recorder of Birmingham was active in many reform movements including that for married women's property rights. (Ray Strachey - op cit p73.) His sister Miss Florence Hill lived in Stapleton and was active in the Suffrage Society.

(18)   Helen Blackburn, op cit p66.

(19)   ibid p.69.

(20)   Mrs Beddoe, *The Early years of The Women's Suffrage Movement*, Bradford on Avon, (1911). (pamphlet in Avon County Reference Library).

(21)   Bristol and West of England Society for Women's Suffrage Annual Reports. These for 1868 - 1882/3, 1890, 1889 - 1900 are in the Fawcett Library, London. Other locally prominent figures listed include the Rev Urijah Thomas, Mr Mark Whitwill, Emily Sturge, Mary Estlin, as well as Mrs Beddoe, the Winkworth and Priestman sisters, Professor Newman and others.

(22)   Marion Ramelson, ch 6 esp. p. 79, Helen Blackburn, op.cit.,
Jo Manton, *Mary Carpenter and the children of the streets, Heinemann (1976)*.

(23)   Mrs Beddoe: op cit.

(24)   Helen Blackburn, p. 110. Rhoda and Agnes Garrett were sisters of Millicent Fawcett and Elizabeth Garrett Anderson.

(25)   Helen Blackburn p.108ff.

(26)   Roger Fulford, *Votes for Women*.

(27)   Roger Fulford op cit.

(28)   For details of the campaign see Marion Ramelson, *The Pellicoat Rebellion* ch 10, Judith Walkowitz, *Prostitution and Victorian Society*, O.U.P. (1980). Josephine E. Butler, *An Autobiographical memoir* and *Personal Reminiscences of a Great Crusade*.

(29)   J. Walkowitz, p. 130.

(30)   M. Ramelson. ch 8.

(31)   Jessie Craigen (pamphlet in Fawcett Library).

(32)   Ray Strachey p. 279.

(33)   R Strachey p. 279-83. M Ramelson p. 92-8.

(34)   M. Tanner, *How the Women's Suffrage Movement was founded in Bristol 50 years ago*, Bristol (1918).

(35)   E. Sturge, *Reminiscences of My Life*, Bristol, (1928).

(36)   Octavia Hill was a prominent worker in charitable housing schemes for working-class people and trained many women housing managers for such schemes. Roger Fulton, in *Votes for Women* mentions Catherine Winkworth's housing schemes.

(37) Bedminster Co-operative Women's Guild minute book, in the possession of the Guild President, Mrs Prewett.
(38) Guild minutes and contemporary printed programme cards.
(39) Mrs Beddoe, op cit.
(40) Pamphlet printed by Bristol and West of England Suffrage Society and in the Women's Suffrage Journal (Oct 1875) (in Fawcett Library and Avon County Reference Library).
(41) D. Large and R. Whitfield, *Bristol Trades Council*, (1873 - 1973), Bristol Branch of the Historical Association, (1973).
(42) M. Ramelson, *Petticoat Rebellion*
      H Goldman, *Emma Patterson*.
(43) S. Bryher.
(44) It is not clear whether this organisation, now called the National Union of Women Workers had a continuous history with the earlier NUWW. If so it had clearly become an organisation of middle-class women working in philanthropy and social work. It later changed its name to the National Council of Women, which still exists nationally.
(45) Gwen Mary Williams, *Mary Clifford* p.144. Mary Clifford was a Poor Law Guardian on the Barton Regis Board which covered the whole eastern sweep of outer Bristol including Barton Hill. It is unclear whether the "we" here refers to the Guardians or the NUWW.
(46) Annie Kenney, *Memoirs of a Militant*, (1908), p. 120. Local reports of the WSPU papers, *Votes for Women* and *The Suffragette*, (1908 - 14).
(47) Bryher, p. 18.
(48) S. Rowbotham and J. Weeks, *Socialism and the New Life*, Pluto Press (1977) Part 1.
(49) Information from Angela Tuckett of Swindon, author of an unpublished biography of her Aunt Enid Stacy *'Our Enid'*.
(50) Bryher Part II p. 6, Rowbotham and Weeks p. 67.
(51) *Angela Tuckett, Our Enid*
(52) Ibid
(53) M.G. Shaw, *Redland High School*.
(54) Angela Tuckett, *Our Enid* ch.3.
(55) Bryher.
(56) Ibid
(57) Ibid Past II p. 40-41
(58) Quoted in Liddington and Norris op cit.
(59) Ibid p. Q
(60) *Red Rag* No 5, (1974), interview with Florence Exten Hann by Sheila Rowbotham.
(61) A programme of the concert is in the Avon County Reference Library.
(62) Sylvia Pankhurst, *The Suffragette Movement*.
(63) *The Suffragette*.
(64) See photograph *Bristol's Other History* p. 124.
(65) Annie Kenney, *Memoirs of a Militant*,
(66) Reports of Bristol Patrols and Police (1916). Avon County Reference Library. Joan Lock, *The British Police Woman: Her Story*. Robert Hale (1979).
(67) Bristol Women's Aid Reports Avon County Reference Library.

People's Housing in Bristol 1870 - 1939

Madge Dresser

Before the First World War in Bristol, there were greater variations in working-class incomes and life styles than there are today. There were those as poor and as outcast as the pauper in Eastville or the prostitute in St Judes. There was the great army of manual workers: the dockers, the carters, the building labourers; the laundry women and factory girls, the chars and the costermongers. Then came the 'artisans', the skilled men who made boots, fixed trains and laid bricks, whose wives often worked unpaid in the home. And above them, in the new offices and department stores of the expanding city, were the white collar workers.

All these people, employed and unemployed, skilled and unskilled, 'rough' and 'respectable' made up Bristol's working class. Housing in Bristol reflected and helped to reinforce the differences between them. There were many different types of housing, and the reputation of each neighbourhood depended in part on the type of housing available.

The best conditions and the highest status were for those who could afford it. The regularly-employed skilled artisan might be able to rent one of the new parlour houses with a garden in Fishponds or Montpelier. His less well-off neighbours might have to share their house with another family.

The unskilled casual worker and those people outside the traditional family unit - the deserted wife, or the childless widower, for example had lower and less regular incomes. These were the people most often relegated to the lodging houses, one-room tenements and tiny courts in central Bristol. For those who could not afford even these, there was one last alternative: the workhouse.

The common lodging houses were one step up from the workhouse, but it was a short step indeed. They were often used by people new to the city:

The only accommodation for workmen visiting Bristol in search of work and with very little money in their pockets were the common doss houses. (Labour Herald, 1910) [1]

According to Reverend Wilkins, an inner-city vicar in the 1890s, most 'bona fide' workers did not stay in Bristol's common lodging houses although about 1000 people a week were said to have passed through the parish of St Jude's alone, the turnover was extremely high. Aside from the newly arrived workers the rest were casual labourers. Wilkins said that the women inhabitants were mostly prostitutes, and he dismissed the men as 'idle vagabonds'. [2] It is difficult to know how far to believe him, as Victorian vicars were often narrow in their judgements. But by all accounts [3] the St Judes doss houses around St Annes and Wade Street were filthy, overcrowded and brutalising places.

There were alternatives. For one thing, not all common lodging houses were quite as dreadful as those found in St Judes. One Bristol journalist of the 1880s writes of a place in Bedminster where, if the conditions were pinched and mean, the atmosphere was cheerful, and the travelling hawkers, flower artists and peddlers there were poor but regular tenants. (4) There were also the strictly-run church hostels such as the YMCA and YWCA. (5) And by 1905, the City of Bristol finally opened a lodging house for men at Wade Street, though it was not at all popular. (6) (Its record book recalls that, during Christmas week, one man who was refused admittance because he was drunk was found on the doorstep the next morning frozen to death.)

On the whole, though, it seems that those who could avoid common lodging houses did so and lodged with private families. Women workers were probably most keen to do this since it was commonly assumed by 'respectable' society that most women living in mixed-sex common lodging houses were 'loose women' and therefore undesirable employees. This assumption was implicit in one Bristol official's report in 1913, which assured the Council that there were

> a considerable number of young females employed in factories (who) are lodging at respectable private homes all over the City and who conduct themselves in a very satisfactory manner. (7)

However, it is by no means clear that there were enough private lodgings available for the influx of women workers who came to Bristol before the First War. Nor do we have a precise idea about what sort of families took in lodgers in order to augment their income. It seems to have been a common practice amongst working-class families, but the evidence is scanty. The interviews of old Bristolians recently conducted by Steve Humphries and Sally Mullen (8) confirm that the taking in of lodgers was common, but the type of lodger taken seems to have varied. For example, one man interviewed was born in 1902 in St Philips Marsh . He thought people in his street took in lodgers, but that

> It would be somebody like the uncle, or someone like that, that would go and live with the family. That's how they used to do it then. I don't think they would have strangers. It would be more or less a family affair. (9)

But the son of a temperance-minded Sussex Place blacksmith recalled that his father took lodgings in Murdock Street in the 1890s when he first came up from Shepton Mallet:

> There were quite a lot of people who did [take in lodgers] . (It would be advertised by word of mouth.) The sort of people that were lodgers varied. Sometimes they were very rough and ready. Another time they were pretty decent. (They were usually strangers come to Bristol for work or people without a family.) (10)

This standpipe is in a court in the Avon St area. Running water was not a feature of every Bristol house until after World War Two. Note the gas lighting on the left of the photo.

Yet according to one lady, the daughter of a clerk of works on a building site, the more respectable families in Redfield would not take lodgers: "We never took in lodgers, not with our crowd".(11)

If the people interviewed are typical we can tentatively conclude that the 'wealthier' working families would view the taking in of lodgers as something the poorer families did. But we can also suppose that the status of lodgers varied widely and ranged from 'respectable' skilled workers and young girls to 'rough and ready' casual workers. It is also of interest to know that at least some people from rural areas found lodgings with relatives in Bristol, since this must mean that traditional family networks had not been completely disrupted by urbanisation.

The poorer worker, especially the casual labourer who needed to live near the crowded city centre because of work, might well take on one or two 'furnished' rooms in a tenement building. The standard of the room and the respectability of the tenant varied from area to area. Some tenants were transient, others brought up families in the one or two rooms they rented. (12) Taking rooms was one way for young married couples to establish themselves as a separate household:

> *A couple just getting married would have one room. And perhaps someone would let them have a front room. Have it like a bedsitting room.(13).*

Of course such makeshift bedsits at the turn of the century would more often than not be without cooking, washing or toilet facilities.

The worst tenements were in the St James and St Judes areas. Some were in back-to-back houses, 'dirty with vermin and cockroaches and unfit to live in'. (14) In 1897, the Corporation registered 400 such tenement buildings, which gave the city the right to inspect these buildings day or night for illegal overcrowding. But, despite the fact that the tenements were the most overcrowded class of housing, few houses were ever inspected, because there was not the staff to do so. And had such houses been effectively inspected, the 'excess tenants' would simply have had to go to equally overcrowded tenements elsewhere in the city.

The rents for furnished rooms varied with the neighbourhood. The boot and shoe workers around Portland Square paid twice the rents charged for rooms near Pennywell Road in the early 1880s. (15) But, higher rents did not automatically guarantee better accommodation, since people were keen to live where they worked and this demand kept up the rents, regardless of the standard of the room.

Even in the twentieth century, there was gross overcrowding and a particularly high death rate in the tenements and courts in the central district of Bristol as well as in the poorer sections of St Philips Marsh and St Georges.

In 1907 a housing reform group led by the local Labour Party exposed the terrible conditions that still existed in 'the healthiest city in Britain'. They found families of nine and ten living in three small rooms and families of three and four packed into one. (16)

Aside from the tenement houses, Bristol's central areas were filled with cottages, some of which dated back to medieval times. In St Judes a number of tiny houses less than ten foot square and built against a wall, lean-to fashion, were inhabited by large families. There were also, in these older districts, narrow 'courts' of two - or three-roomed cottages which could be entered only through a passage from the street. Many of these courts had charming names - Paradise Row, Waterloo Buildings, etc. - which belied the fact that they were often in a filthy state and were seen by local health officials simply as breeding grounds for disease.

The report by the 1907 Bristol Housing Reform Group gives us a graphic picture of two such courts:

> 1. *'Labourer, living in 3 roomed house, with wife and 6 children. House dark and dismal; very dark entrance to court; living room over a cellar littered up with rubbish accumulated for years, causing a fearful smell. People living in house intermittently ill in consequence.'*
> 2. *'Four two-roomed houses shared 1 water-tap which was in a shed at the entrance to court, some distance from the houses and was open to the children of the district. Tenants complained of this being used for offensive purposes.'* (17)

Today both the best and the worst courts have all been demolished but their memory lingers on. One lady born in 1897 recalls living in a Hotwells court (Jones's Buildings). The six three roomed cottages (one kitchen, two bedrooms) shared two outside toilets and one cold-water tap between them. This was not exceptional yet if one figures an average of six people per house, there must have been some 36 people dependent on one cold-water tap and 18 people using one toilet. And inside these same cottages there was little room to spare, as this same lady remembers:

> *Three in a bed - 'Get over, I'm sleeping in the middle' (!) Kids of today don't know what it's like - and then they call it the good old days.* (18)

The courts began to be cleared by the turn of the century. In 1890 official records list 320 courts housing 2000 people, but by 1912 only 165 courts housing 1000 people remained. (19)

But their demolition is not a story of unalloyed progress. For something was lost when the best of the courts were cleared. For one thing, not all courts were notorious breeding grounds of disease and 'vice'. Some courts were quiet,

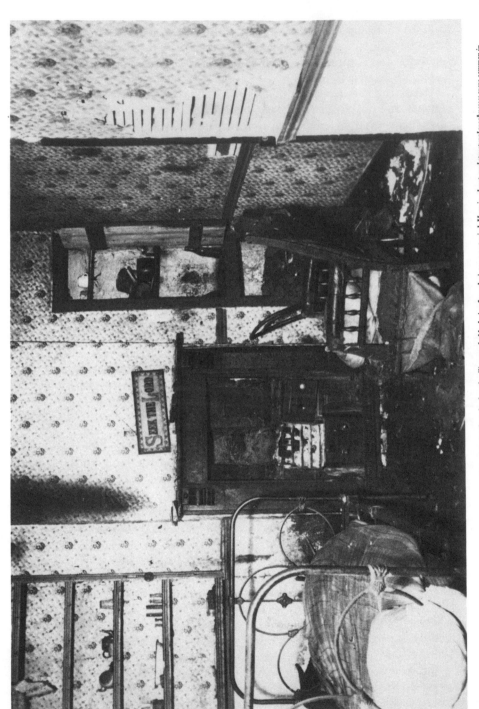

A rare interior shot of a slum dwelling, probably dating from the inter-war period. Vermin, damp and structural weaknesses were common in

picturesque (20) and even 'respectable', housing skilled as well as unskilled workers. Some were clean and relatively comfortable by the standards of the day, such as the well-kept courts in Bridewell which were cleared to make way for the new Police Station.

These courts had pictures hanging on the walls, whilst the courts in York Place had small gardens. Some must by virtue of their age alone have been of architectural interest. One court in Redcliffe boasted a cottage that had been decorated inside and out in the 1870s by a ship's carpenter. This unknown artist covered 'walls, doors, skirting bords, lintels and shutters...with oil paintings of...Neptunes and Mermaids, satyrs and nymphs, mythological heroes and heroines, gods and goddesses'. It was demolished a decade later as part of a church-sponsored slum clearance scheme. (21)

The other point about the courts was that they were popular with working people if not with health officials and developers. One local vicar of the 1880s put the case for the courts in a way which recalls the present-day conflict between residents of pre-fabs and the City Council:

> (Despite the growing number of new workmen's cottages there was) nothing answerable to these little courts where a man can get a little house of his own and where a man can say, 'This is mine for myself'. There is nothing like that to be got elsewhere and I have no doubts that numbers of people like those little places because they have no common staircases to quarrel over. (22)

The large size of families, common before the First World War, meant that even the newer terraced houses were often grossly overcrowded by today's standards. Even when houses weren't shared by two families, even when lodgers were not taken in, the four to six rooms characteristic of the better working-class homes did not go far when there were so many children in the family.

Most of the large numbers of new working-class houses built between 1870 and 1904 were small, plain-fronted houses, built directly onto the pavement, such as those inhabited in Easton, St George and Bedminster. Some of these were jerry-built and, as one critic put it, 'little better than boxes with slate lids'.(23)

In some houses there was not enough room to enable everyone in the family to eat around the table at one sitting. Many people recorded in the Bristol Interviews complained of the constant noise and hubbub and the lack of privacy and often commented on the efforts parents made to ensure that modesty in such close quarters was maintained. The lack of fuel for lighting meant that poorer families were confined to one room where the oil lamp was kept burning. Before the war, as one Bristolian informs us, 'If you wanted to go to bed early, you'd go up and just go to bed, take a candle. No lamps or nothing'.(24)

One lady born in Windmill Hill at the beginning of this century was asked if she shared a bedroom as a child:

> *Now, you said something there! The (3) boys used to sleep in the small back room and, us girls, we had one big bed. That was me, Dorothy, Kathleen, Ethel - oh and Lily she left home...and we didn't use it of a ordinary bed - we used to lie in it longways 'cause there was some at the top and some at the bottom. So we was squabbling, we was squabbling over this, so we eventually laid longways..."*(25)

It is striking that within living memory sanitary facilities in many working-class areas in Bristol were so poor. Despite the efforts of energetic health officials, sanitation even in some of the more newly-developed neighbourhoods left much to be desired. For example, a two-bedroom parlour house in a 'very respectable road', in Bedminster (Stanley Street), had an outside toilet built over a cesspool. Another Bedminster resident born in 1898 reports that he had seen:

> *...these holes in the ground...it was they never used to have any drains up here years ago. They never had anybody come up with ashes...They used to have cess-pools and they used to clean them out every so often.* (26)

And even in those areas which were connected to the sewerage system, sharing outside toilets seemed to be the norm. Functioning water closets were a rarity according to the Bristol Interviews. As one man patiently explained: 'No, you didn't have flush (toilets). That was posh if you had flush sanitation'. (27)

The better working-class houses had cold water taps in the scullery but hot water was not so readily obtained: 'We used to boil up the water, heat the water in the boiler and then tip it out into a big zinc bath'. (28)

The weekly bath, let alone the weekly laundry must have been a major undertaking in such circumstances.

Vermin was widespread in the older and poorer housing. (29) Rats were a nuisance in these areas, particularly near the docks. The son of a Barton Hill candlemaker and cotton mill worker recalls bugs in the walls and in the beds in their brick-built terraced parlour house. The son of an engineer and 'housewife', born in St Philips Marsh in 1905, remembers:

> *There was bugs in the wall, warn't there. We used to get a needle and pull them out of the wall when we was kids...We used to go and get needles and stick them in the walls and find them.*(30)

Many households were lousy. The presence of lice did not necessarily denote poor housekeeping, as children could and did despite the vigilant

This untitled photo gives a good feel of the density and darkness of the old Bristol courts. Note the open drainage in the foreground.

efforts of their mothers, catch lice at school: 'We were clean, but we had lice.'(31)

A thought should be spared for those women who had the immensely difficult task of keeping their houses clean. Many working-class women worked outside the home (Bristol had one of the highest proportion of women workers in the country), many others took in laundry, or did other types of home or factory work. ('But for this army of working women, families would at once be swept into the workhouse'). (32) They did this in addition to their housework which, before the days of labour-saving devices and well-planned houses, was a physically exhausting task, particularly considering the frequent pregnancies (and miscarriages) typical of those pre-birth-control days.

The bad design and lack of amenities of many working-class houses meant extra housework. For instance, a common feature of cheap housing in Bristol was a front parapet into which rain-water would collect and eventually seep through into the house. 'There are more rainy ceilings in Bristol,' complained one Barton Hill resident, 'than in any other place I was ever in.' (33)

At the lower end of the working-class housing market, bare stone or wood floors also meant hard work for the women and girls. As one lady who lived in Hotwells and Clifton remembers:

'No...we never had no lino, gosh. And another time we'd have sand; we used to bash up a sand stone...and we'd take it home and we'd get a hammer and beat it up and then used to sprinkle the sand over the top of the stones...to make it look a little better.(34)

One man from St Philips, when asked if there were carpets in his childhood home, replied:

Carpets! Good God, they used to have to scrub the boards, the bare boards. It was a luxury if you got a sack to put down as a mat. What they used to do, the women used to scrub the passage out and then they used to throw red sand down. Buy the red sand in the shops. There was never no carpets. (35)

But a man from Easton, son of a soldier and an unofficial midwife, does remember rugs and curtains in his pre-war childhood home. (36) And the lady in Redfield, whose family felt 'a cut above the neighbours', tells us of the lino, rugs and piano in her parents' sitting room. (37) Most respectable of all perhaps was the lady who lived in Kingsdown in a three-bedroom parlour house which had not only carpets but lace curtains and gas lights. (38)

At a time when most working wages were meagre, personal spending habits and management skills could make a big difference to a family's standard of living. And this fact partly explains the enthusiasm of many working women and men for the Temperance Movement. Very heavy drinking (what we would probably call widespread alcoholism today) was still a feature of working-class

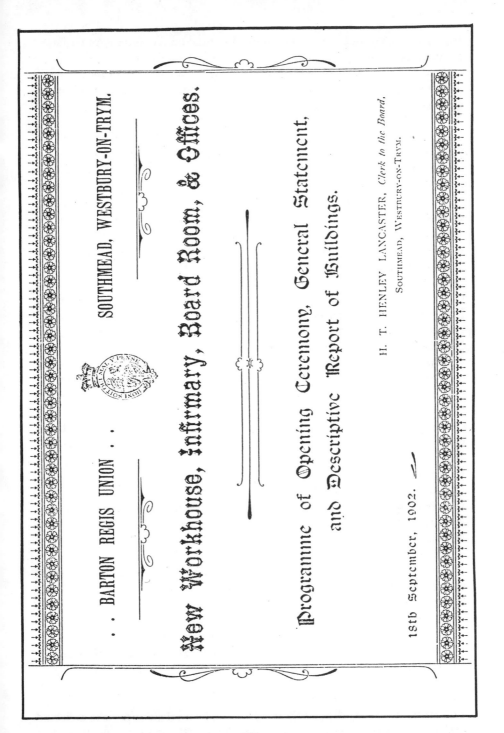

.. BARTON REGIS UNION ..

SOUTHMEAD, WESTBURY-ON-TRYM.

New Workhouse, Infirmary, Board Room, & Offices.

Programme of Opening Ceremony, General Statement, and Descriptive Report of Buildings.

H. T. HENLEY LANCASTER, *Clerk to the Board*,
SOUTHMEAD, WESTBURY-ON-TRYM.

18th September, 1902.

life in the 1880s and 90s, although by this time better water supplies and a general rise in living standards meant that it was on the decline. (39) But on a limited and often irregular wage, the choice was often between a convivial pint and smoke, or a rug on the floor. As one Bristolian, born in 1903 in Sussex Place, explains:

> *Dad (a blacksmith) didn't drink (and)...he smoked very little so that mother was able to do things that other people weren't able to do...we had carpets and curtains and (cheap) wallpaper. (40)*

Yet even the most careful families could have problems meeting the rent. According to the 1885 Royal Commission on Working Class Housing, many of the newer 'artisans' and workmens' dwellings were let out at rents beyond the means of most workers. (41) Although average wages did rise between 1885 and 1914, rents kept apace; and the irregularity of work along with the low wages made it particularly hard for many people to meet the rent.

Of course there were families who never failed to pay the rent, but a surprisingly wide range of people in the Bristol Interviews remember bad times when their parents had to 'give the landlord the bump', or 'put 'im in the Promised Land and say we'd pay 'im next week'. (42)

Pawning clothes in order to meet the rent seems to have been a regular occurrence amongst a number of unskilled families, (43) but there is not the evidence to be more precise about what proportion of families depended on pawning to pay the rent. We do know that a very high number of Bristolians (some 10,000 people out of a population of 387,000) were on some form of poor relief in 1910. (44) More than half of these lived outside the workhouse on a weekly dole of two to five shillings a week at a time when even the worst slum tenement room cost 1s.6d. a week.

Amongst the poorest families then, the percentage of 'moonlight flits' must have been relatively high compared to the rest of the working population. And as the 1885 Royal Commission reports, those landlords who had 'defaulting tenants' recouped their losses by charging higher rents to their other tenants. (45)

For the lower-paid worker, rent day was often a time of crisis. One man, raised in St Philips Marsh, recalls that his family's landlord, a local garage owner, collected the rents on his several houses personally.

> *He'd get paid sometimes. Then he would want to throw us out and then we would pay so much off. The rent was about five shillings a week. We worried about being thrown out of our home (into the workhouse) all the time. (46)*

That same man recalls that there was a woman on their street who collected her neighbours' belongings in a pram and took them to the pawn shop each week, getting ½d. commission on each bundle. All this suggests that a distinctly communal 'hand to mouth' approach to rent payments existed in some poorer neighbourhoods, 'anything to get a few bob 'til pay day'.

The better-paid skilled worker might find that a slack season, slump or industrial dispute might put him behind in his rent. The family of the respectable Sussex Place blacksmith for example was a regularly paying tenant, and even possessed a rent book. The only time he could not pay the rent was when he went out on strike. His son can remember the rent collector

> *shouting and bawling at us and saying that we should be thrown out if we didn't pay the rent and all that. But fortunately, the strike didn't last long.* (47)

In contrast today, where less than 15% of the population rents from a private landlord, the overwhelming majority of working people before the First War rented their accommodation.

So far we have looked at what the houses were like. But when we talk about working-class housing in Bristol we are not only talking about how most people lived, but also about how some people made money. Up to the early 1900's, housing was a major form of investment. It is with housing as a money-making enterprise that I would now like to deal.

Who owned working-class housing?

In the years between 1861 and 1888, thousands of people from rural areas came into Bristol. (48) The resulting rise in Bristol's population was reflected in the increase in house building. In the 1860s middle-class areas such as Redland and Cotham grew; by the 1870 and 80s, working-class house building began in earnest in Montpelier, St George, Bedminster, Easton, Totterdown, and elsewhere.

Now there were all sorts of people making money from working-class housing. First was the property developer. These developers (who were often builders) either sold the houses they developed 'on spec' as an investment property to be rented out, or they kept their houses and rented them out themselves. By the 1890s, working-class house building was booming. It seemed such a good investment (as safe as houses) when even the older slum properties in St Judes yielded at least a 7 - 10% return.(49)

There were no building bye-laws in Bristol until the 1890s and so many of the suburban developments were hurriedly run up, and a number were jerry-built. For example, houses in Lincoln Street, Richmond Street and Morton Street in the Redfield/Barton Hill area were erected with 'sun baked (as a distinct from kiln baked) bricks' on slate and tar foundations.

The typical speculative developer was said to have been a man 'with very little to lose'. He was often financed by solicitors, investing on behalf of their clients' estates. (50). These clients could be wealthy but the majority of investors do not seem to have been particularly rich.

In fact, by the turn of the century, anybody who could raise a third of the purchase price of a small house (say, about one third of £175) could obtain a mortgage and become a houseowner. Building societies did not come into their own until the 1920s, and so, before the War, such small-time purchasers would often finance the rest of their purchase by 'farming' the house out to a tenant. This tenant would in turn pack in the maximum number of paying sub-tenants into each room. Alternatively, the mortgagees might live in part of the house and sublet the rest out themselves - some small builders were apparently able to become owner-occupiers in this way. (51)

The whole system of house-farming encouraged overcrowding, particularly with the older properties. It also discouraged landlords from spending money on repairs. Often, when houses were let and sub-let, it was difficult to know just who the real landlord or landlady was. But it was a set-up which enabled a number of people to take a cut of the profits.

For example in St Judes, near the Castle Green public house one 'landlady' rented a six roomed house in the 1890s for just under seven shillings a week. She kept three rooms for herself and let the others 'furnished' at three shillings each per week. She got her own rooms rent-free plus 2s.3d. each week in addition. Another landlady in the same area did not live on the premises. She sub-let a house which she rented for seven shillings a week for twice that amount on the furnished-room system.(52)

The wealthier investor might engage an estate agent or solicitor to handle his or her property. Rents on some of the most wretched and notorious slum courts in Bristol - the Irish quarter and red light district at Quakers Friars - were collected in the 1880s by an agent for an absentee landlord. (53)

Other investors might make an indirect profit on slum housing by putting their money in a company employing casual labour at low wages, or into a bank which offered mortgages on old properties. Like those who invest in Barclay's today, they were accused by one local reformer of 'putting their consciences in commission'. (54)

There was one more party who stood to make money from working-class housing. That was the ground landlord. For not all land in Bristol was sold outright to developers or houseowners. A sizeable proportion of land in Bristol was only leased to housebuyers.

Who were the great landowners - the true landlords - of Bristol? The whole story has yet to be pieced together, but we do know that much of South and West Bristol (Bedminster and Ashton and Knowle) was owned by Sir Greville Smythe's family of Ashton Court.

Much of the oldest inner-city property was in the hands of various church bodies (such as vestries, the Dean and Chapter , the Ecclesiastical Commissions), or such charities as the Merchant Venturers, the Merchant Taylors and the Charity Trustees. Another large owner of land in central Bristol was the Corporation of Bristol itself. For example, the city owned sizable parts of St Clements and St Agnes parishes as well as the area around and including College Green. (55)

House-farming was rife in church-owned property. According to the 1885 Royal Commission, many church owned houses were 'used for the worst purposes', (i.e. as brothels and gambling dens). Both charities and church bodies protested that they were unhappy that slums and brothels abounded on their properties, but professed they were powerless to interfere with the leaseholder if he refused to be bought out.

But there is evidence to suggest that the churches and charities could have done more than they did to improve conditions on their properties, from which, after all, they were deriving a tidy income. As one reformer wrote:

It is not edifying to think that some of the most dilapidated dwellings in the poorer parished of the city belong to church vestries and that in some instances appeals for restoration meet with a deaf ear.(56)

Although most of the speculative development of working-class houses on the North and East of the city was on freehold property, some of the newer houses were on leasehold property. The ground rents increased as property values rose, and ground rents were notoriously high in Bristol in the 1880s compared with other cities.(57) Naturally the developer would pass on the ground rent in the purchase price of leaseholds, and the leaseholder would in turn charge his tenants a higher rent. And, by this process, working-class tenants were left to finance ground landlords of Bristol.

The forty years before World War I was a time of upheaval and change in the city's housing stock. We have already noted the growth of new working-class suburbs on the outskirts of the old city. These new houses were tenanted by workers able to leave the increasingly crowded city centre, workers who often earned enough to meet tram or omnibus fares to their workplace.

In some cases the new suburbs engulfed pre-existing hamlets and villages. In one area at least suburban development displaced earlier settlers. This was the case when the area around the new parish of St Agnes was developed for working-class housing. Before 1870, this was still largely 'old garden ground' in the parish of St Pauls which has been let out in small allotments. According to a contemporary source , the tenants of these allotments

gradually put chimneys into their toolhouses and converted them into dwellings. So long as they did not attempt to put on a second storey they were not interfered with and thus arose a curious race of squatters...of whom the last trace disappeared in 1885...(58)

At its height, some 500 or more people, breeding fowls, ducks and pigs, and famous for 'monster vegetables', reportedly lived in this colony.

> *Towards this convenient no man's land, the roughest class of the population gravitated; and [dog and pigeon fancying] prize fighting, and even cock-fighting were their favourite amusements.* (59)

The tiny dark shacks inhabited by these people were so low that it was said a passerby could put his hand through the chimney and lift the pot off the fire. (60) Most shacks had one room, but they were not as standardised as the monotonous if more respectable developments which were to follow. In at least one of these shacks - a three-room affair inhabited by a family of eight, the windows were filled in with odd bits of stained glass in varieties of styles from old summer houses and ancient dwellings'. (61)

This colourful group reminiscent of pre-industrial days met its end as speculative development encroached. By the early 1880s

> *the squatters **after some resistance** had to give up their cabins, as the land was let on ground rents for the new streets of houses into which mechanics and others from congested districts streamed as soon as they were built. (Emphasis mine)* (62)

At the same time that the population increased and new suburbs sprang up, the central areas of Bristol were being 'cleared out', for both new streets and for more profitable uses than that of working-class dwellings. The emergence of a central business district, with its warehouses, offices and throughfares came at the expense of the poorest section of the community. (63)

For example, the construction of Victoria Street meant the end of the old alleys and houses in New Temple Street. Railway development also cleared 'hovels in Pile street' and elsewhere around Temple Meads. The new police buildings at the Bridewell and the Industrial School in Silver Street were erected on the ruins of working-class dwellings. Houses in the old Pithay area were demolished to make way for New Union Street, and what is now the 'old' red-brick Wills Building in Bedminster replaced old unhealthy courts.

In addition, public health legislation, granting wider powers to the City Council from 1890, meant that many courts and houses were closed on health grounds in the years leading up to the First War. The tenants evicted were not rehoused by the city but were left to fend for themselves.

Those who could, moved out to the new suburbs, but a core of people too poor to move out were left in the centre or pushed into those 'transitional areas between the centre and the more affluent suburbs'. The worst housing conditions persisted up to (and beyond) 1914 in St Judes, St James, parts of St Philips, South Bedminster, Hotwells Redcliffe and the Temple.

Bedminster, one of Bristol's oldest working class areas, was very overcrowded by 1914 and many houses were in need of repair. Many houses which were officially closed on health grounds would be occupied by families in times of acute shortage, for example, after the First World War.

To make matters worse, the housing market showed signs of decline just after 1900. As early as 1904 the Bristol Medical Officer of Health called attention to the slump in working-class house building and by 1914 noted that, as house values fell

> *landlords have in many instances, lost all financial interest in their housing...Mortagees are allowed to take possession and...they frequently have no desire to undertake the responsibilites of the landlords.* (64)

So not only were fewer new houses built, but existing working-class dwellings were allowed to fall into disrepair at an unprecedented rate.

Virtually no working-class dwellings, were built after 1904 and the housing market in Bristol and elsewhere collapsed almost completely when Lloyd George introduced a tax on land holdings in 1910. The crash in the housing market helped to produce an acute housing shortage by 1914, a shortage which reached crisis point in the years after the Great War.

Housing reform before 1914

Towards the end of the last century, a few leading Bristol families (notably the Fry, Wills and Charles Hill families) tried to provide for those workers squeezed out by urban development in the city centre. But these philanthropists would back only self-financing housing schemes which would yield investors a small but steady return. As a result of their deference to market forces, the strictly-run 'model tenement houses', which they built in Jacob Wells Road and Brandon Hill on the site of the present day Council blocks in the 1870s, were too expensive for the unskilled worker most in need of centrally-located accommodation.(65)

In an attempt to reach the lower-paid worker, two other middle-class reformers, the Winkworth sisters, set up a housing management scheme in Dowry Square which was modelled on Octavia Hill's work in the London slums. (66) (Hill's idea was that with lots of 'visiting' by lady rent collectors, along with prompt repairs and equally prompt eviction of those in arrears, slum conditions would be improved along with the aspirations and habits of the tenants).

But, by 1885, all these schemes housed less than 1,000 of Bristol's 220,000 inhabitants. (67) The efforts of housing reformers, operating as they did on laissez-faire principles, barely scratched the surface of what was beginning to be recognized nationally as 'the housing problem' (68)

In Bristol, as elsewhere in Britain, housing reform became an increasingly popular issue during the 1880s. The sensational series on 'The Homes of the Bristol Poor' in *The Bristol Mercury* stirred many consciences. So too did the

Courts, often without direct access to the street, were the oldest form of working class housing development in Bristol. Insanitary and overcrowded, court housing often dated back to before the industrial revolution.

East Bristol floods which in 1882 and 1889 made many people homeless, amid much publicity. (69)

Bristol's Town Council, in the pre-War period, was largely Conservative. Conservative councillors, with one eye on the rate-paying electorate, declared it was not the role of the Council to subsidise housing. The Liberal opposition (led by the non-conformist Wills family) had long pressed for a wide range of social reforms, but they were also wary of too much municipal spending.

There were only four Labour councillors by 1900 and so their support for higher spending on municipal services did not count for much. But Labour members did form a very active, if tiny, ginger group within the Council, and their influence in raising issues exceeded their actual voting strength as the century progressed.

Growing public concern over the increasing numbers made homeless by street clearance schemes forced the Council to heed its reformist minority and build its first council dwellings before the First World War. Between 1901 and 1907 tenement blocks designed to house 74 artisan's families were built in East Bristol. (70) (In Mina Road, two of these two-storey blocks are still used by the Housing Department.)

Labour activists referred contemptuously to these grim buildings as 'brick-built barracks' and campaigned for more council housing of a better standard. The Council did go so far as to build four parlour houses in Fishponds (where land was cheaper) in 1907, but conservatives of both major parties were quick to condemn their high cost, and were able to end the experiment because it was not self-financing. (71)

Whilst the Council dithered over the expense of municipal housing, the general housing shortage in Bristol was rapidly worsening. Not only were no new working-class houses being built after 1904 because of the collapse of the housing market, but more and more people were being made homeless by Council clearance schemes. Thanks to new powers granted to the City under the 1909 Housing and Town Planning Act, slum clearance reached a peak between 1909 and 1915. During these years, over 1,200 houses had been closed, and those evicted were not rehoused. (72)

These people could not afford the high rents of the new suburban housing. And even owners of low-rent houses in the central districts 'declined to let their houses to people so evicted' (from slums). For example, those people turned out of condemned   housing in Gas Lane, St Philips, 'flocked into a court in Jacob Street...' only to be turned out by the landlord there. (73)

The housing crisis in Bristol and several other cities helped to fuel more general labour unrest. One local Labour councillor, writing just after the 1912 Bristol Dock Strike, cited the housing situation as a major cause of trade union militancy:

To clear slum areas and pull down insanitary dwellings is good, but only insofar as you provide healthier dwellings for people to live in is it of any use. Then again, as to overcrowding, the homes of the poor are being inspected and where worse overcrowding exists it must cease. This all means added difficulty to the struggling poor. (74)

Bristol Council now began to receive deputations and petitions from progressive Liberals and Labour supporters pressing for more municipal housing. By 1914, the local inspector of housing told the Council plainly that

The congestion is becoming very acute, and if private enterprise cannot provide houses for the working classes, it will be necessary for the municipality to do so.

Resistance to the idea of government intervention in housing was beginning to weaken. Even within Conservative circles (at national as well as local level), intervention was seen as a temporary necessity given the collapse of the house-building industry.

But though the Conservatives (and right-wing Liberals) were reluctantly prepared to provide municipal housing, they made it clear that such dwellings should be reserved only for the poorest slum dweller, and only until the market recovered. In contrast Labour and left-wing Liberal reformers in Bristol wanted a more comprehensive housing policy whereby high-quality homes would be supplied to a wide range of the working population. And Labour's supporters and Liberals outside the Council stressed that Bristol's current housing problem was not simply one of slums, but also that 'of narrow mean streets, of jerry-built housing; ill-designed and lacking in the 'convenience' which every house should possess.' (75)

The Council on the other hand, as one reformer wrily noted, all profess to be very anxious to do something about the housing shortage but 'it must not cost the ratepayers anything.' (76) Private philanthropic efforts (such as the 44 garden cottages let by the Bristol Garden Suburb Ltd in 1913 at a rate of 2½% return) were clearly not solving the problem. And as pressure from trade union and womens' groups mounted in the following year, the Council was forced to consider a scheme for four Corporation cottages in Bedminster and Stapleton Road. This scheme was supported by trade unions and left-wing Liberals and included plans for municipal tram lines.

Liberals within the Council were probably emboldened to propose the scheme largely because the Council had recently received a £50,000 legacy from a local philanthropist for the express purpose of building garden-suburb style cottages. (The proposed scheme was to cost £50,000.) However, the more right-wing elements in the Council managed to get even this scheme shelved, once war broke out in 1914.

During the War of course, house building and repairs were generally suspended. It is likely that the shortage of housing was further exacerbated by the influx of workers into Bristol to work in war-related industries. (This was certainly true of Avonmouth, where the housing shortage for employees of the National Spelter Works was especially severe.) In 1915 rent control was instituted by Parliament, but this did not cure the problem as it did not provide new houses.

The one housing scheme partially implemented in Bristol during the war began as a housing co-operative sponsored by left-wing Liberals and such Labour activists as Ernest Bevin, Ben Tillet and Councillor Frank Sheppard. Their Avonmouth Garden Suburb Scheme was intended to provide accommodation for workers at the strategically important Spelter Works and Docks at Avonmouth. The Avonmouth project featured such innovative proposals as communal laundries, kitchens and nurseries for working women; shops, sportsgrounds and community social centres; as well as a coordinated transport scheme. But Sir Napier Miles, who owned the land on which houses were to be built, objected at the eleventh hour to shops and other nonresidential buildings in the scheme. In the end, the project in its original form was abandoned and the much needed houses were built years later. These 150 houses, which according to one source were 'sub-standard', formed the basis of Bristol's Penpole Estate. (77)

By the War's end the country as a whole was 'ready' for Government intervention to solve the housing shortage. There were several reasons for this new readiness. For one thing the years of 'war-time socialism' had set a precedent for state involvement in social and economic activity and so had undermined opposition to government involvement in housing. For another, the shortage was by now extremely acute. There was genuine fear felt by those in power that the failure to grant some measure of social reform could spark off serious social unrest. There was also an equally genuine, if shortlived, feeling of community (a sort of prototype of the Dunkirk spirit) which made it unfashionable for the Press and public figures to dismiss the needs of the millions of working people whose contribution to the War had been so impressive.

Council Housing and the Council Tenant

A Quick Look at Housing Policy or How History Repeats itself.

Bristol's first council estates were begun under the generous national housing subsidy of 1919. Within the year, building had begun at Hillfields Park (Fishponds), Sea Mills, Shirehampton, Knowle, and St Johns Lane. Yet by 1921, the increasingly conservative Coalition Government at Whitehall called for cutbacks in public spending to counter the worsening economic climate and high interest rates. The new housing subsidy was cut and local authorities were being pressed to sell off as many of the newly-built houses as possible and this only a year after they had been built! (78)

Just under 1,200 houses were completed in Bristol under the 1919 'Addison' subsidy - not enough to stem the worsening housing crisis. Private house building (in a bad way before the War) had been further hit by the post-War slump. Because rent increases were forbidden under the 1915 Rent Control Act, builders had no incentive to build cheap houses to let, especially when building materials and skilled workers were still in short supply.

By 1923, the housing shortage was worse than ever and a 'House Famine' campaign was launched by a wide range of political and community groups. In Bristol that year there was a well-attended rally at Colston Hall and a stream of letters and petitions pressing for more council housing. Conditions in Bristol were desperate: 3,000 houses, previously condemned as unfit, were now being inhabited for lack of alternatives. And the shortage affected the skilled as well as the unskilled worker. (Estimates varied but probably well over 15,000 dwellings were needed simply to meet the immediate shortage in Bristol)

The new Conservative government, shaken by the widespread disquiet responded by instituting small subsidies, aimed mainly at encouraging private enterprise to build houses for owner occupiers (although a small number of subsidies were granted to local authorities. This subsidiary to private builders did little to house working-class families (between 1923, and 1929 only some 1,600 Council houses in Bristol were built under this Act) who traditionally lived in rented accommodation, especially since the government also decontrolled rents that same year resulting in many evictions. In Bristol alone, over 500 eviction orders were granted in 1923, representing an increase of two-thirds over the previous year.

In 1924, the first Labour Government came briefly to power and devised a new housing subsidy specially geared to assisting local authorities to build for a wider range of working-class families. Although less generous than the earlier Addison programme, the 'Wheatley Act' (named after the then Minister of Health) did enable Councils to build houses to let at lower rents than was previously possible.

Most of the council houses built during the 1920s and early 1930s were built under this Act. In Bristol over 7,000 houses were financed by it. But by 1933 the National Government (a Conservative - dominated Coalition) ended the Wheatley subsidy on grounds of economy and restricted new subsidies to the rehousing of the very poor. Between 1933 and 1939 Bristol Council was restricted to the rehousing of 3,500 slum clearance families, at a time when building costs were at their lowest.

The inter-war period also saw the building society mortgage come of age. By the mid-thirties Bristol's private house builders were building exclusively for the growing numbers of owner-occupiers in Henleaze, Bishopston and the other new suburbs on the outskirts of town.

The BRISTOL GARDEN SVBVRB Shirehampton

Bristol's Liberal Reformers provided a very limited number of high standard working class houses before World War One and few workers could afford them.

By the outbreak of World War II enough new houses had been built. (By 1939, 14,500 Council houses had been built. 3,000 private houses had been built with assistance from Government subsidies and over 17,000 houses had been built without government subsidies by private enterprise.)

Rents and Tenants

The new council estates did not supply the needs of the majority of working-class families. Corporation houses in the early 1920s were well built with spacious interiors and large gardens. But the rents were dear and sub-letting forbidden on pain of eviction. As a result, only the highest paid worker could afford them. Clerks, artisans and a sprinkling of reporters and teachers comprised the first tenants on the Fishponds estate. Gradually, some lower-paid workers, mainly dockers and labourers were also housed on these early Bristol Corporation estates, mainly at Shirehampton, St Johns Lane and Fishponds.

Workers with large families found particular problems paying the rent, especially as they had to meet the additional costs of rates, tram fares and furniture. As the economy slumped in the summer of 1920, many new Corporation tenants went into arrears. The Housing Committee reduced rents despite initial opposition from the Government, but rents in Bristol were still quite high compared to those of other authorities and even other authorities found they had arrears problems.

By 1922, tenants at Fishponds and Knowle had organised into tenants groups to press for further rent and rates reductions. That same year, a local Liberal weekly *(The Bristol Observer)* reported on the hardships suffered by Council tenants, quoting a local vicar from Fishponds who declared that:

The trade depression now rampant everywhere had resulted in much unemployment on the estate and (he) himself..had come across some harrowing cases of poverty and actual starvation. (79)

Unemployment remained chronic throughout the decade, and by 1923 local housing officials complained that there was 'scarcely a single house' on the new council estates where unauthorised sub-letting did not occur. In the circumstances the Council had to turn a blind eye to sub-letting, particularly on the estates housing the largest proportion of unskilled workers. Even so, a quarter of Shirehampton tenants and almost a third of those at St Johns Lane were in arrears by 1924. As the General Strike of 1926 and the continuing coal strike affected jobs and wages, the position of council tenants took a turn for the worse. By October that year, just under half of the 800 or so Corporation tenants in Bristol were in rent arrears! During that same year, the Conservative Government chose to reduce the council house subsidy. This had the result of raising rents of council houses all over the country (though in Bristol rent rises were restricted to the Sea Mills estate, which had a high proportion of parlour houses). Even before the cuts, Councils had been told to put more of their money into rehousing slum-clearance families, and a special more generous subsidy had been made available for this purpose as early as 1923. Tenements were built at Lawfords Gate and Eugene Street between 1923 and 1925 to rehouse *some* of those displaced in a slum-clearance scheme. The blocks were built on expensive central sites. And in order to keep rents low enough for poor families facilities were spartan - there were, for example no bathrooms. Yet not all of those who were rehoused found they could afford the rents of even those tenements.

Meanwhile, the development of council estates on the outskirts of Bristol went on, as building costs continued to fall from the high levels of 1920. A good proportion of the 1,100 families who left these estates by 1928 did so because they had problems paying the rent. Tenants groups at Knowle and Fishponds, continued to press for rent reductions, but without success. Conservatives at local and national levels saw one way out of the rent problem: housing costs had to be further cut so that cheaper houses could be built and let at lower rents. There was no question in their minds of advocating subsidy increases! Thus, the search for experimental building materials was not simply a technical exercise but was a political manoeuvre aimed at keeping down Government spending.

Alternatives to brick-built houses were therefore particularly encouraged by the Conservative Governments. Profiteering by building suppliers (along with the preference of most suppliers to cater to the needs of private, more profitable building schemes) meant that bricks were often in short supply or unduly expensive. Conservative politicians were reluctant to legislate against such 'trade rings'. In addition, new materials often needed less skilled labour and skilled labour was often scarce, expensive, and well organised. For all these reasons, alternatives to bricks were an attractive proposition to the ministry. But although attractive in theory, experimental building materials were (then as now) problematic in practice. The concrete houses at Horfield, for example proved particularly ugly and unpopular. And the steel houses built in Knowle and Speedwell were minor disasters for the Council (and major disasters for the tenants living in them. These houses were notorious for their malfunctioning fireplaces and condensation problems.)

The Conservatives of the 1920s like their counterparts today, wanted to minimize Government spending on housing, limiting it where possible only to the very poorest and most alienated sections of society. Slums according to one prominent Tory of the time (Kingsley Wood), were not only a 'festering sore', but also 'nurseries of crime and disease'. Their goal was to leave housing provision for the vast majority of working people to private enterprise, even though private enterprise was clearly neither willing or able to supply it.

Where they did build council houses, Conservative-dominated Councils prompted by Whitehall, cut corners in the name of economy. For this reason council housing declined in quality from the late twenties up to the outbreak of the second war. Yet the same Conservative (and 'Citizens Party') councillors, who had pared down the housing budget at every opportunity, were the first to condemn council estates for their monotonous appearance.

The Council Estates Between The Wars

The council estates were planned with high hopes. In Bristol, left-wing Liberal and Labour Councillors advocated municipal trams, gardens and a wide range of community facilities. But by the time the plans were actually carried out, these same progressive politicians found themselves defending the bleak and under-resourced estates from Tory and tenant alike.

As early as 1920, the chairman of Bristol's Housing Committee concluded, on practical grounds, that 'houses had to come before planning.' The same pragmatism led the growing labour majority on the council increasingly to view the provision of estate amenities as 'unrealistic'. Reformers on the left had struggled so hard to secure Council approval for the houses themselves that anything more must have seemed like an'optional extra'.

The result of the 'houses before planning' policy meant that for years the estates went without the most basic facilities. Roads remained unpaved for months on end; transport, where it existed at all, was inadequate and expensive. At Seamills there were no shops until 1929 (where the first houses were built in 1920), nor were there any at Knowle or Horfield until the 1930s. Tenants were dependent on travelling hawkers who could charge what they liked for food, furniture and other necessities. One source claimed that many new residents fell prey to high pressure salesmen flogging overpriced encyclopedias and furniture under the then new hire purchase arrangements. People would be enticed into signing agreements which committed them to expenditure they could not really afford. [80] Less sinister figures might include the fishman on the motorbike, the travelling hairdresser, and the ladies who made dresses and crocheted hats in their homes. [81] Libraries and schools were slow in coming to the estates. [82] Robert William Harvey and Joan Goodere both remembered being schooled in old army huts. [83] And for the whole of the twenties, there was not one cinema, social centre, or pub provided on a Bristol Corporation Estate.

Nor were medical services adequate. It seems to have been the pracice for non-resident doctors to take rooms in a council house for use as a surgery. This led to overcrowding, and according to an official Bristol report:

> During epidemics and often in normal times, patients have had to queue for attention, sitting on the stairs in some instances or even out in the garden. [84]

The distance from hospital must have also caused tenants much worry especially in the absence of cheap and frequent bus and tram services or public telephones.

It does seem that whatever amenities there were were due to the persistent campaigning of the tenants themselves, with and without the support of individual Labour Councillors. Electricity - first considered by the Council in 1919, but vetoed by the Ministry on ground of expense - was not installed until after a campaign by tenants in 1928. And even then the installation took nearly a decade to complete. Because council housing was in part financed from the rates and from taxes (the rest coming from council-house rents), housing officials' number one priority was to safeguard the 'public investment'. Because of this approach, the needs of the tenant often took second place. Public spending on social services such as housing, was a new-fangled idea, subject to many attacks (especially from ratepayers' groups). Also, there was the longstanding argument, still current, that it was the 'slum dweller' who created the slum and who would abuse council housing. (And other workers, it was implied, would and should be able to find private housing once the economy returned to normal)

In a sense then, council housing was always on trial, and so was the council house tenant. Then, as now, council tenants in Bristol found themselves subject to rules and regulations which did not apply to those who could afford to own their own homes or even, in many cases, to those who rented privately.

The most blatant example of this, was the refusal by Bristol Council, in the bitter days after the General Strike, to allow a Labour Party meeting on a Corporation estate. But there were also more subtle restrictions on tenants, many of them implicit in the selection procedure. The 'model tenant', it seems, was assumed by Bristol housing officials to be a clean-living and right-minded family man who was to be diverted from the pub, protected against subversion, advised on housekeeping and tempted into horticulture.

For example, the ban on sub-letting (which was in practice widely ignored but which could always be invoked at the discretion of the Housing department) coupled with the ban on working from the home, imposed serious constraints on the earning power, and thus the status, of women within the family. True, some women on council estates did work at Wills, despite the high travelling costs this involved; and, true, some took in laundry to cope with the high rents and their childrens' appetites.[85] But, compared with the wide array of jobs (however low-paid) available to women living in the city, the isolation of the estates must have proved difficult.

Visiting by housing welfare officers (themselves women and underpaid) also intruded on the privacy and self-respect of many tenants and their wives. For, although it is undeniable that these 'visitors' often helped families from the poorest housing cope with the unfamiliar facilities in the new council houses they were often resented for their 'slumming mentality' and for 'poking their noses everwhere, even in our cupboards'.(86)

Not only were tenants' housekeeping standards vetted, but so were their gardening skills, all in the interests of ensuring they were not abusing the public money 'lavished' on them. As one Bristol Tory Councillor advised:

[If only tenants will] live up to the new conditions in which they find themselves. If they will treat their dwellings, garden, privet hedges and grass verges with proper respect, life would be that much more pleasant for them and they will save the Housing Committee much anxiety and a great deal of money.(87)

By 1930, the local official in charge of council estates could declare (with evident relief) that:

Contrary to the prophecies of pessimists, picture rails are used, and baths are not misused. Gardens are generally very well cultivated and prove of great service to the tenants. Horticultural societies have been formed on the large Estates and the results obtained are most gratifying...(88)

Of course, as more and more people from the worst slums in central Bristol were moved out to the suburbs, during the 1930s, the membership lists of the Horticultural Societies began to wane. People from the inner city were often casual labourers with unsteady incomes and 'rough' reputations. With the influx of these poorer workers, the official role of the welfare visitor and the rent collector loomed larger then ever. And it is from the late twenties onwards, that council estates begin to be designated in the popular imagination as 'rough' (Knowle West) or 'respectable' (Sea Mills).

The suburban estates were furnished with *family* houses; single people did not, it seems officially exist. Moving from one council property to another was a very bureaucratic affair and, since most people wanted to move closer into the city centre, was usually impossible. In any case, 'transfers' were granted at the discretion of the Housing Committee, and so were repairs and alterations.

This was Housing for the people, but not by the people, and in such a hostile political climate, Bristol's estates were never built with adequate transport links or social facilities. And not enough houses were built, so slum and substandard housing persisted up to the middle of the twentieth century and beyond. Decent, well-equipped housing could not be provided unless interest rates and building materials costs were controlled. Yet there was not the political will to do either of these. Also because the Labour friends of council housing were always on the defensive, they tended to be less imaginative than they might have been overlooking the potential of centrally-located housing, the renovation (as opposed to the clearance) of slum property, and the provision of less conventional dwellings than the parlour cottage. (Their attitude was largely due to the fact that when such alternatives were proposed (usually by Conservatives or right-wing Liberals) they were presented as cheap substitutes for a substantial and high standard council house programme).

And finally, because council housing had always to prove it was giving ratepayers and the Ministry "value for money," its administration was less accountable to the tenants than it need have been. Not enough emphasis has been given to the way in which the isolated location and bureaucratic administration of council estates undermined the communal life and independence of their residents. These criticisms must be set against the fact that council housing undeniably provided thousands of families with a better standard of accommodation than they have ever known, and for better or worse, the development of council estates and the clearance of old neighbourhoods have probably changed Bristol, and all of our lives, as much as anything else this century.

(1)   *The Bristol Labour Herald*, 3 April 1910

(2)   H.J. Wilkins, 'What Can I Do To Promote The Better Housing of The Poor In Bristol.' (1893) This pamphlet is in The Avon County Reference Libary (local collection). Wilkins was the vicar of St Judes, Bristol.

(3)   See Wilkins and also The wonderfully readable "Homes of the Bristol Poor', extracts from *The Bristol Mercury* (1884), available Avon County Reference Library. *The Royal Commission on the Housing of the Working Classes* vol II (1885) has a special section on Bristol and is full of interesting material. It is available at the University Library but you might be able to order it from the Reference Library.

(4)   *Homes of the Bristol Poor* (see note 3), chapter on Bedminster

(5)   Helen Mellor *Leisure and the Changing City 1870 - 1914*, 1976 is about Bristol and discusses middle-class activity on behalf of the poor.

(6)   See the *Minutes of the Sub-Committee on the Housing of the Working Classes*, 1905 - 1914. This sub-committee ran the hostel (now the Salvation Army Hostel, I believe). The *minutes* are available at the Bristol City Records Office (Council House) where the equally interesting *Reports of the City Engineer* (good on building activity in the city) and *The Medical Officers of Health* (good on housing and health) can also be consulted.

(7)   *Minutes of the Sub-Committee on the housing of the Working Classes*, 30 Sept 1912, 21 Oct 1912, 24 Jan 1913, 13 May 1913. There was a large 'surplus' of women over men in Bristol in the late 19th and early 20th centruy, some 30,000 by 1914 according to calculations done of the basis of the 1911 census.

(8)   The Bristol Interviews with old Bristolians were done in 1980 by Dr Steve Humphries and Sally Mullen they are not yet fully transcribed or catalogued but will eventually it is hoped to be available at the Reference Library. I should like to thank Steve Humphries for allowing me to look at his manuscripts and for asking respondents some questions at my request.

(9)   *Bristol Interviews*, M5

(10)   *Bristol Interviews*, M7, M8

(11)   *Bristol Interviews*, F37

(12)   Bristol Interviews Wilkins op cit. *The Royal Commission on the Housing of the Working Classes* (1885) Vol II., 229 - 31. *The Board of Trade Report*, an Enquiry into working-class rents, housing and retail prices and standard notes of wages in the U.K. (1908), cd 3864; *Report* of the Joint Select Committee on the Housing of the Working Class (1902), cd 325. The University of Bristol research library restricts entry to non students but you might be able to obtain the Royal Commission's findings and the other reports mentioned here by way of the 'interlibrary loan system' at the Central library.

(13)   *Bristol Interviews* M5

(14) *Report* of the Bristol Housing Reform Committee (1907) in the Frank Sheppard collection in the City of Bristol Record Office.

(15) *Homes of the Bristol Poor*, Board of Trade *Report* (1908).

(16) See note 14.

(17) *Ibid*

(18) Bristol Interviews, F.11

(19) As reported in the *Western Daily Press* 29 October 1912 (Bristol Central Library).

(20) *Homes of the Bristol Poor* 15, 66; Board of Trade Report (1908); Royal Commision (1885)

(21) *Homes of the Bristol Poor*, 69.

(22) *Royal Commission* (1885) vol II 218 - 9

(23) *Bristol Labour Herold* 2 April 1910 op cit. see also the *Annual Reports* of the Bristol Garden Suburbs Ltd in Bristol Central Reference Library - esp the report of the conversation between Dr. Eliza Dunbar and Elizabeth Sturge (the two founders of the Bristol Garden Suburb Company, an early housing association).

(24) *Bristol Interviews*, M5, M7.

(25) *Bristol Interviews*, F30.

(26) *Bristol Interviews*, M8.

(27) *Bristol Interviews*, M56; F 17 F4, M32 M15 etc also "Discussions on housing with the Mothers of the Barton Hill Mothers School, *Unpublished Ms*, (1918) uncatalogued collection of the Barton Hill University Settlement, Bristol.

(28) *Bristol Interviews*, M7; M32.

(29) See *Reports* of the (Bristol) Medical Officer of Health c 1900 - 1914; Bristol Interviews eg M15, M47, F54 etc.

(30) *Bristol Interviews*, M5.

(31) *Bristol Interviews*, M39.

(32) See *Homes of the Bristol Poor*, P17; Bristol Interviews, F.W. Lawrence *Local Variation in Wages*, 1899, 82-3; Bristol's Sweated Trades (1908) (Exhibition) (Bristol Reference Library). The type of home work mentioned in the sources included tailoring, hawking, match making, pipe making washing, stick chopping; fancy mat making. See also Bristol Interviews, sp. F36, F11, M15 for mention of gardening work and unofficial midwifery.

(33) Barton Hill discussion paper, *opcit* (1918).

(34) *Bristol Inverviews*, F11.

(35) *Bristol Interviews*, M5.

(36) *Bristol Interviews*, M15.

(37) *Bristol Interviews*, F37, M20.

(38) *Bristol Interviews*, F19.

(39) *Homes of the Bristol Poor*, p 96 - 7 in which the author declares that local police surveys confirmed his impression in a decline in drunkeness. See also H. Mellor *Leisure and the Changing City op cit.*

(40) *Bristol Interviews*, M7.

(41) Royal Commission Vol II, pp 217 - 291, 221 -2, 228, 232, 234. Neil Ferguson 'The attack on the slums in Bristol and Nottingham 1890 - 1915' unpublished M5, 1979, 12. See note 12 and *Report* of the Housing Reform Committee (1907)

(42) *Bristol Interviews*, M32.

(43) *Bristol Interviews*, M15, M47, F30, M8 etc.

(44) Social Services Committee of the Bristol Adult School Unions, 'Facts of Bristol's Social Life,' (pamphlet, 1914) in Bristol Trades Council Collection at Bristol Record Office, 32080. See also *Royal Commission* Vol II 1884, 234 ad Hunt *op. cit.*

(45) *Royal Commission*, Vol II, 219

(46) *Bristol Interviews*, M5

(47) *Bristol Interviews*, M7

(48) *Royal Commission* Vol II 1885 pp 232 - 3. H.A. Shannon and E. Grebenik, *The Population of Bristol* (1943).

(49) Wilkins, *op. cit.*

(50) *Royal Commission Vol II 1885, 229*

(51) *op. cit* 1229 - 31

(52) Wilkins *op cit.*, Royal Commission Vol II (1885) esp 221, 229 - 31.

(53) *Homes of the Bristol Poor* 10 - 12

(54)   *Wilkins* op cit.
(55)   *Royal Commission* vol II 1885, 219
(56)   *Homes of the Bristol Poor*, p65 *Royal Commission* Vol II 1885, 228, 231-4
(57)   *Royal Commission* Vol II (1885) 221 and 222. By 1899 they seem to have fallen relative to other cities according to F.W. Lawrences' *Local Variations in wages* (1889), 82 3, 49
(58)   Clifton College, *The History of St. Agnes Parish* (1890). Thanks to Sally Mullen for providing me with a copy of the relevant pages of this booklet.
(59)   *Ibid* also *Royal Commission* Part II (1885) 217
(60)   *Ibid*
(61)   *Homes of the Bristol Poor*, 34 - 5
(62)   *Ibid*
(63)   *Ibid*.
(64)   *Report* of the (Bristol) Medical Officer of Health 1914. See also *Reports* of the (Bristol) City Engineer, 1900 - 1914.
(65)   *Royal Commission* (Part II) 1885, 2, 6, 7 Avonmouth's *Dictionary of Bristol* (1906) under 'Housing of the Poor'. Mellor op cit. 27
(66)   *Ibid*.
(67)   *Op cit.* 238
(68)   See for example J. Mearns *The Bitter City of Outcast* London (1883), or read G. S. Jones *Outcast London* (1976).
(69)   See for example *Western Daily Press* 12 March 1889 and also the *Bristol Times and Mirror* 12 March 1889. Thanks to Mrs Claire Kimber for the loan of photocopies of newspaper features from an exhibition she previously prepared on the history of St Pauls, Bristol.
(70)   *Report* of the Joint Select Committee on the Hours of the Working Classes (1902) C d 325. Avonmouth's *Dictionary of Bristol*, *Report* of the Bristol City Engineer, 1906.
(71)   *WDP* 29 October 1912.
(72)   Cf *Reports* of the (Bristol) City Engineer 1904 - 1914. Ferguson MS, op cit, 19, *report* of the Bristol Housing Reform Group 1907.
(73)   *WDP* 29 October 1912.
(74)   F. Sheppard, 'Labour's Unrest and some of its causes' (1912) in the Sheppard Collection.
(75)   *Bristol Labour Herald 2 April 1910*
(76)   'Facts of Bristol's Social Life' (1914), *op cit.*
(77)   Letters and documents in the Sheppard Collection, Ferguson *'Working class Housing in Bristol and Nottingham,'* (phd University of Oregon, 1971).
(78)   See Madge Dresser Summerbell *'Bristol's Housing Policy 1919 - 1930'* (Msc, University of Bristol 1980) on my chapter in M. Daunton, ed *Councillors and Tenants* (1983) for most of the references used. I shall footnote only direct quotes in this section.
(79)   *The Bristol Observer* 11 March 1922 7, available Bristol Central Reference Library, as are all local newspapers used in this study.
(80)   Mr. Norman Rich who kindly supplied this information was a cub reporter in 1926 for the *Western Daily Press* of which he later became news editor.
(81)   *A Bristol Childhood* 6, 7 Thanks too to Mrs Joan Goodere for the information on Sea Mills. The best written source on Bristol's estates during this period is R. Jevons and J. Madge, *Inter war Housing Estates (1946), available Avon County Reference Library.*
(82)   Mrs Joan Goodere
(83)   *Robert William Harvey, A Bristol Childhood* (1976), 6-7.
(84)   *Report* of the Bristol Corporation Housing Department 1955, recalling the pre-war situation on Council estates. Mrs Goodere reported that at Sea Mills there was a resident doctor who lived in a private house on the estate.
(85)   From a pamphlet in the uncatalogued archives of the Barton Hill University Settlement in Bristol.
(86)   Jevons and Madge, 95, *Up Knowle West*, Knowle West T.V. Workshop and Bristol Broadsides (1977) 28.
(87)   Sir John Surdish in the *Bristol Times and Mirror* 24 Jan 1927.
(88)   Bristol Corporation Housing Department, 'Bristol Housing 1919 - 1930'. (nd but c. 1931).